MO🌓N

SPOTLIGHT

CALIFORNIA DESERTS
CAMPING & HIKING

TOM STIENSTRA • ANN MARIE BROWN

How to Use This Book

ABOUT THE CAMPGROUND PROFILES

The campgrounds are listed in a consistent, easy-to-read format to help you choose the ideal camping spot. Here is a sample profile:

Site name and number →

General location of the site in relation to the nearest major town or landmark →

Icons noting activities and facilities at or nearby the campground

Rating of scenic beauty on a scale of 1–10 with 10 the highest rating

Symbol indicating that the site is listed among the author's top picks

1 SOMEWHERE USA

Scenic rating: 10

south of Somewhere USA Lake

BEST

Each campground in this book begins with a brief overview of its setting. The description typically covers ambience, information about the attractions, and activities popular at the campground.

Campsites, facilities: This section notes the number of campsites for tents and RVs and indicates whether hookups are available. Facilities such as restrooms, picnic areas, recreation areas, laundry, and dump stations will be addressed, as well as the availability of piped water, showers, playgrounds, stores, and other amenities. The campground's pet policy and wheelchair accessibility is also mentioned here.

Reservations, fees: This section notes whether reservations are accepted, and provides rates for tent sites and RV sites. If there are additional fees for parking or pets, or discounted weekly or seasonal rates, they will also be noted here.

Directions: This section provides mile-by-mile driving directions to the site from the nearest major town or highway.

Contact: This section provides an address, phone number, and website, if available, for each site.

ABOUT THE ICONS

The camping icons are designed to provide at-a-glance information on activities, facilities, and services available on-site or within walking distance of each campground.

- 🏃 Hiking trails
- 🚲 Biking trails
- 🏊 Swimming
- 🎣 Fishing
- 🚤 Boating
- 🛶 Canoeing and/or kayaking
- ❄ Winter sports

- ♨ Hot Springs
- 🐾 Pets permitted
- 🛝 Playground
- ♿ Wheelchair accessible
- 🚐 RV sites
- ⛺ Tent sites

ABOUT THE SCENIC RATING

Each campground profile employs a scenic rating on a scale of 1 to 10, with 1 being the least scenic and 10 being the most scenic. A scenic rating measures only the overall beauty of the campground and environs; it does not take into account noise level, facilities, maintenance, recreation options, or campground management. The setting of a campground with a lower scenic rating may simply not be as picturesque that of as a higher rated campground, however other factors that can influence a trip, such as noise or recreation access, can still affect or enhance your camping trip. Consider both the scenic rating and the profile description before deciding which campground is perfect for you.

ABOUT THE TRAIL PROFILES

Each hike in this book is listed in a consistent, easy-to-read format to help you choose the ideal hike. From a general overview of the setting to detailed driving directions, the profile will provide all the information you need. Here is a sample profile:

Map number and hike number →

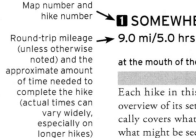

1 SOMEWHERE USA HIKE

Round-trip mileage → **9.0 mi/5.0 hrs**

Round-trip mileage (unless otherwise noted) and the approximate amount of time needed to complete the hike (actual times can vary widely, especially on longer hikes)

Difficulty and quality ratings

at the mouth of the Somewhere River ←

General location of the trail, named by its proximity to the nearest major town or landmark

BEST (

Each hike in this book begins with a brief overview of its setting. The description typically covers what kind of terrain to expect, what might be seen, and any conditions that may make the hike difficult to navigate. Side trips, such as to waterfalls or panoramic vistas, in addition to ways to combine the trail with others nearby for a longer outing, are also noted here. In many cases, mile-by-mile trail directions are included.

Symbol indicating that the hike is listed among the author's top picks

User Groups: This section notes the types of users that are permitted on the trail, including hikers, mountain bikers, horseback riders, and dogs. Wheelchair access is also noted here.

Permits: This section notes whether a permit is required for hiking, or, if the hike spans more than one day, whether one is required for camping. Any fees, such as for parking, day use, or entrance, are also noted here.

Maps: This section provides information on how to obtain detailed trail maps of the hike and its environs. Whenever applicable, names of U.S. Geologic Survey (USGS) topographic maps and national forest maps are also included.

Directions: This section provides mile-by-mile driving directions to the trailhead from the nearest major town.

Contact: This section provides an address and phone number for each hike. The contact is usually the agency maintaining the trail but may also be a trail club or other organization.

ABOUT THE ICONS

The hiking icons are designed to provide at-a-glance information on the difficulty and quality of each hike.

The **difficulty rating** (rated 1–5 with 1 being the lowest and 5 the highest) is based on the steepness of the trail and how difficult it is to traverse

The **quality rating** (rated 1–10 with 1 being the lowest and 10 the highest) is based largely on scenic beauty, but also takes into account how crowded the trail is and whether noise of nearby civilization is audible

ABOUT THE DIFFICULTY RATINGS

Trails rated 1 are very easy and suitable for hikers of all abilities, including young children.

Trails rated 2 are easy-to-moderate and suitable for most hikers, including families with active children 6 and older.

Trails rated 3 are moderately challenging and suitable for reasonably fit adults and older children who are very active.

Trails rated 4 are very challenging and suitable for physically fit hikers who are seeking a workout.

Trails rated 5 are extremely challenging and suitable only for experienced hikers who are in top physical condition.

MAP SYMBOLS

Expressway	Interstate Freeway	Airfield
Primary Road	U.S. Highway	Airport
Secondary Road	State Highway	City/Town
Unpaved Road	County Highway	Mountain
Ferry	Lake	Park
National Border	Dry Lake	Pass
State Border	Seasonal Lake	State Capital

CALIFORNIA DESERTS CAMPING

BEST CAMPGROUNDS

◖ Waterskiing
Moabi Regional Park, **page 25**
Los Alamos, **page 26**
Havasu Landing Resort and Casino, **page 31**

There is no region so vast in California — yet

with fewer people - than the broad expanse of the California deserts. Joshua Tree National Park, Death Valley, Mojave National Preserve, Anza-Borrego Desert State Park - each of these respective areas has distinct qualities, separate and special, yet they are also joined at the edges.

On a fall evening, you can take a seat on a ridge, overlooking hundreds of square miles of landscape, and just look. Every few minutes, you'll find, the view changes. It is like watching the face of someone you care for, one minute joyous, the next pensive, then wondrous, then mysterious.

The desert is like this, always changing the way it looks, just as the sunlight changes. The reason is that as the sun passes through the sky, its azimuth is continuously changing. In turn, that causes a continuous transformation in the way sunlight is refracted through the atmosphere and across the vast landscape. So, especially at dawn and dusk in spring and fall, the desert looks different from minute to minute. For those who appreciate this subtlety, the desert calls to them in a way that many others do not understand.

Joshua Tree National Park features a sweeping desert landscape edged by mountains and peppered with the peculiar Joshua tree. It is best known by most as the place where the high desert (Mojave Desert, 4,000 feet elevation) meets the low desert (Colorado Desert). This transition creates a setting for diversity in vegetation and habitat. The strange piles of rocks often appear to have been left there by an ancient prehistoric giant, as if chipped, chiseled, and then left in rows and piles.

The national park is far different than Mojave National Preserve. The highlights here are the Kelso Dunes, a series of volcanic cliffs and a forest of Joshua trees. It is remote and explored by relatively few visitors. The Mojave is a point of national significance because it is where three major landscapes join: the Sonoran Desert, the Colorado Desert, and the Mojave Desert.

Death Valley is the largest national park in the lower 48 states, yet there are only nine campgrounds. Because of the sparse nature of the land, campers should arrive self-contained; that is, equipped with everything they need. Some of the highlights include Badwater, at 282 feet below sea level the lowest point in the United States. Yet also in the park is Telescope Peak, towering at 11,049 feet. Crazy? Oh yeah.

When viewed from a distance, in between is a vast terrain that seems devoid of vegetation. The sub-sea-level salt flats indeed can seem like a bunch of nothing. But they are linked to barren, rising mountains, Eureka Dunes, and surrounding vastness everywhere.

Anza-Borrego Desert State Park is so big that it seems to stretch forever - and that is because it does. The park covers 600,000 acres, the largest state park in California. The landscape features virtually every type of desert terrain, but most obvious are canyons, badlands, and barren ridges. In spring, the blooming cholla can be impressive. This is habitat for the endangered desert bighorn, and seeing one can be the highlight of a lifetime of wildlife-viewing. The nearby Salton Sea, created in an accident from a broken dike, provides one of the most distinct (and strange) lakes on earth and is one of the largest inland seas in the world.

Throughout this country, campgrounds are sprinkled in most of the best spots. Some are extremely remote. Some consist of nothing but flat parking areas. Some are simple staging areas for OHV riders, and some serve as base camps for weekend parties. Somewhere amid all this, a place like no other, you will likely be able to find a match for your desires.

So if you see somebody sitting on an overlooking ridge at dusk, watching the changing colors of the landscape as if it were created from the palette of an artist, well, don't be surprised. When it comes to beautiful views, the changing colors of the emotion of the land, it doesn't get any better than this.

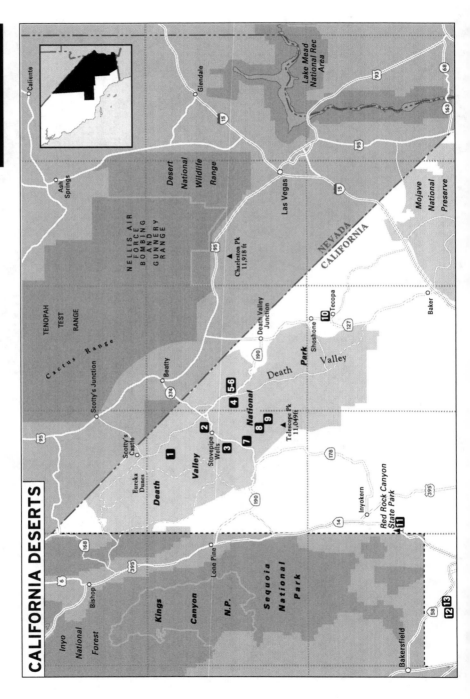

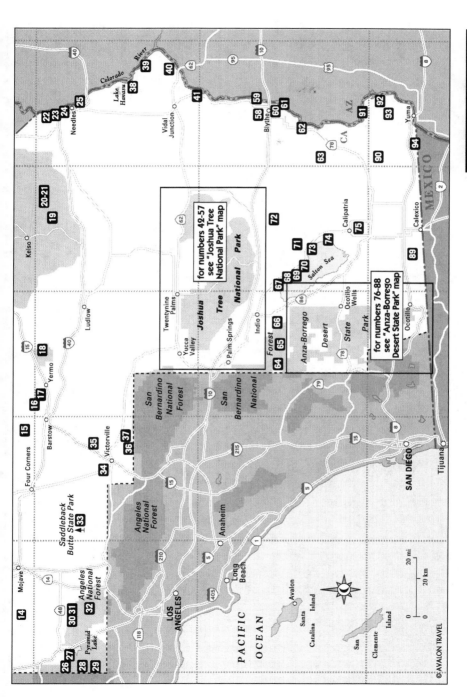

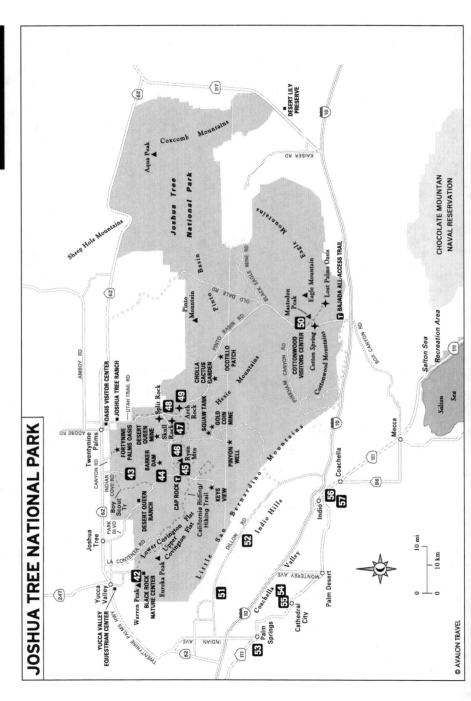

JOSHUA TREE NATIONAL PARK

ANZA-BORREGO DESERT STATE PARK

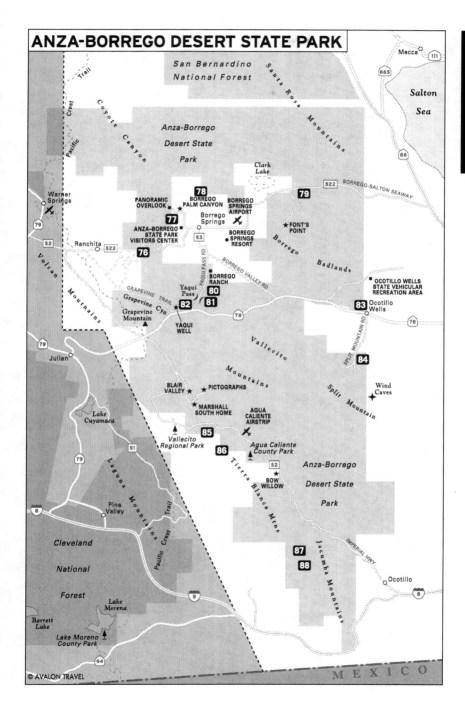

San Bernardino National Forest

Santa Rosa Mountains

Mecca

111

863

Salton Sea

Pacific Crest Trail

Coyote Canyon

Anza-Borrego Desert State Park

Clark Lake

S22

BORREGO-SALTON SEAWAY

86

Warner Springs

79

S2

Ranchita

S22

PANORAMIC OVERLOOK

78 BORREGO PALM CANYON

BORREGO SPRINGS AIRPORT

79

77

Borrego Springs

ANZA-BORREGO STATE PARK VISITORS CENTER

S3

BORREGO SPRINGS RESORT

FONT'S POINT

76

Borrego

Badlands

OCOTILLO WELLS STATE VEHICULAR RECREATION AREA

GRAPEVINE TRAIL

YAQUI PASS RD

BORREGO VALLEY RD

BORREGO RANCH

Volcan Mountains

Grapevine Cyn

Yaqui Pass

82

80

81

78

Ocotillo Wells

83

78

Grapevine Mountain

YAQUI WELL

Vallecito

SPLIT MOUNTAIN RD

84

79

Julian

Mountains

Split Mountain

Wind Caves

Lake Cuyamaca

BLAIR VALLEY

PICTOGRAPHS

MARSHALL SOUTH HOME

AGUA CALIENTE AIRSTRIP

S1

85

Vallecito Regional Park

86

Agua Caliente County Park

S2

Anza-Borrego

79

BOW WILLOW

Desert State

Laguna Mountains

Pacific Crest Trail

Tierra Blanca Mtns

Park

8

Pine Valley

Cleveland

IMPERIAL HWY

87

Jacumba Mountains

National

88

Forest

Lake Morena

Ocotillo

8

Barrett Lake

Lake Morena County Park

94

M E X I C O

CAMPING

1 MESQUITE SPRING
🏃 🏕 ♿ 🚐 ⛰

Scenic rating: 7

in Death Valley National Park

Mesquite Spring is the northernmost and often the prettiest campground in Death Valley, providing you time it right. If you are a lover of desert beauty, then you must make this trip in late winter or early spring, when all kinds of tiny wildflowers can bring the stark valley floor to life. The key is soil moisture, courtesy of rains in November and December. The elevation is 1,800 feet. Mesquite Spring campground is within short range of two side trips. It is five miles (past the Grapevine Entrance Station) to Ubehebe Crater, a scenic point, and four miles to Scotty's Castle, a historic building, where tours are available.

Campsites, facilities: There are 30 sites for tents or RVs up to 30 feet (no hookups). Picnic tables and fire grills are provided. Drinking water, flush toilets, and a dump station are available. Some facilities are wheelchair-accessible. Leashed pets are permitted.

Reservations, fees: Reservations are not accepted. Sites are $12 per night, plus a $20 park entrance fee that is valid for seven days. Visitors may pay the entrance fee and obtain a park brochure at the Furnace Creek, Grapevine, Stovepipe Wells, or Beatty Ranger Stations. Open year-round.

Directions: From Furnace Creek Visitor Center, drive north on Highway 190 for 19 miles to Scotty's Castle Road. Turn right (east) and drive 33 miles (just before the Grapevine entrance station and three miles before reaching Scotty's Castle) to the campground entrance road on the left. Turn left and drive two miles to the campground.

Contact: Death Valley National Park, 760/786-3200, fax 760/786-3283, www.nps.gov/deva.

2 STOVEPIPE WELLS
🏃 🏊 🏕 ♿ 🚐 ⛰

Scenic rating: 4

in Death Valley National Park

Stovepipe Wells is on the major highway through Death Valley. The RV sites consist of an enormous asphalt area with sites simply marked on it. There is no shelter or shade. But note: Get fuel here because prices are usually lower than at Furnace Creek. An unusual trail is available off the highway within a short distance; look for the sign for the Mosaic Canyon Trail parking area. From here you can take the easy one-mile walk up a beautiful canyon, where the walls are marble and seem as if they are polished. Rock scramblers can extend the trip for another mile. The elevation is at sea level on the edge of a large expanse of Death Valley below sea level.

Campsites, facilities: There are 18 sites for tents only and 200 sites for RVs of any length (no hookups). Picnic tables and fire rings are provided at the tent sites. Drinking water, restrooms with flush toilets and coin showers, dump station, swimming pool (extra fee), camp store, and gasoline are available. Some facilities are wheelchair-accessible. Leashed pets are permitted at campsites only.

Reservations, fees: Reservations are not accepted. Sites are $12 per night, plus a $20 park entrance fee per vehicle that is valid for seven days. Open mid-October through mid-April.

Directions: In Stovepipe Wells Village, drive west on Highway 190 to the signed entrance (just before the general store) on the right.

Contact: Death Valley National Park, 760/786-3200, fax 760/786-3283, www.nps.gov/deva.

CAMPING

3 EMIGRANT
🏃 🐕 ⛺

Scenic rating: 4

in Death Valley National Park

The key here is the elevation, and Emigrant, at 2,100 feet, is out of the forbidding subzero elevations of Death Valley. That makes it one of the more habitable camps. From the camp a good side trip is to drive south 21 miles on Emigrant Canyon Road, then turn east on Upper Wildrose Canyon Road for seven miles, the last two miles a rough dirt road. That done, you come to the trailhead for Wildrose Peak, on the left side of the road at the parking area for the Charcoal Kilns. The trail here climbs 4.2 miles to the peak, with awesome views in the last two miles; the last mile is a butt-kicker.

Campsites, facilities: There are 10 sites for tents only. Picnic tables and fire rings are provided. Drinking water and flush toilets are available. Campfires are not permitted during the summer. Leashed pets are permitted at campsites only.

Reservations, fees: No reservations are accepted and there is no camping fee; however, there is a $20 park entrance fee per vehicle that is valid for seven days. Open year-round.

Directions: In Stovepipe Wells Village, drive eight miles southwest on Highway 190 to the campground on the right.

Contact: Death Valley National Park, 760/786-3200, fax 760/786-3283, www. nps.gov/deva.

4 FURNACE CREEK
🏃 🐕 ♿ 🚐 ⛺

Scenic rating: 5

in Death Valley National Park

This is a well-developed national park site that provides a good base camp for exploring Death Valley, especially for newcomers. The nearby visitors center includes Death Valley Museum and offers maps and suggestions for hikes and drives in this unique wildland. The elevation is 190 feet below sea level. This camp offers shady sites, a rarity in Death Valley. It's open all year, but keep in mind that the daytime summer temperatures commonly exceed 120°F, making this area virtually uninhabitable in the summer.

Campsites, facilities: There are 136 sites for tents or RVs up to 35 feet (no hookups), and two group sites for up to 10 vehicles and 40 people each. Picnic tables and fire rings are provided. Drinking water, flush toilets, dump station, and evening ranger programs are available. Campfires are not permitted during the summer. Some facilities are wheelchair-accessible. Leashed pets are permitted at campsites only.

Reservations, fees: Reservations are recommended mid-October through mid-April at 877/444-6777 or www.recreation.gov ($10 reservation fee). Sites are $12–18 per night (includes reservation fee), plus a $20 park entrance fee per vehicle that is valid for seven days. Group sites are $50 per night. Open year-round.

Directions: From Furnace Creek Ranch, drive one mile north on Highway 190 to the signed campground entrance on the left.

Contact: Death Valley National Park, 760/786-3200, fax 760/786-3283, www. nps.gov/deva.

5 TEXAS SPRING
🏃 🐕 ♿ 🚐 ⛺

Scenic rating: 2

in Death Valley National Park

Although this camp is slightly more protected than Sunset camp, there's limited shade and no shelter. The lower half of the campground is for tents only. It is open only in winter. The upper end of the camp has trails that provide access to the historic springs and a viewing area. The nearby visitors center, which features the Death Valley Museum, offers maps and suggestions for hikes and drives. The lowest point in the United States, Badwater, set 282 feet below sea level, is to the southwest. This camp has one truly unique feature: bathrooms that are listed on the National Historic Register.

Campsites, facilities: There are 92 sites for tents or RVs of any length (no hookups). Picnic tables and fire rings are provided. Drinking water, flush toilets, and a dump station are available. Campfires are not permitted in the summer. Some facilities are wheelchair-accessible. Leashed pets are permitted.

Reservations, fees: No reservations are accepted. Sites are $14 per night, plus a $20 park entrance fee per vehicle that is valid for seven days. Open mid-October through mid-April.

Directions: From Furnace Creek Ranch, drive south on Highway 190 for 0.25 mile to the signed campground entrance on the left.

Contact: Death Valley National Park, 760/786-3200, fax 760/786-3283, www.nps.gov/deva.

6 SUNSET

Scenic rating: 4

in Death Valley National Park

This camp is another enormous section of asphalt where the campsites consist of white lines for borders. Sunset is one of several options for campers in the Furnace Creek area of Death Valley, with an elevation of 190 feet below sea level. It is advisable to make your first stop at the nearby visitors center for maps and suggested hikes (according to your level of fitness) and drives. Don't forget your canteen—and if you're backpacking in Death Valley, never set up a wilderness camp within 100 yards of water.

Campsites, facilities: There are 1,000 sites

for RVs of any length (no hookups). Drinking water, flush toilets, and a dump station are available. Campfires are not permitted in the summer. Some facilities are wheelchair-accessible. Leashed pets are permitted at campsites.

Reservations, fees: No reservations are accepted. Sites are $12 per night, plus a $20 park entrance fee per vehicle that is valid for seven days. Open mid-October through mid-April.

Directions: From Furnace Creek Ranch, turn south on Highway 190 and drive 0.25 mile to the signed campground entrance and turn left into the campground.

Contact: Death Valley National Park, 760/786-3200, fax 760/786-3283, www.nps.gov/deva.

7 WILDROSE

Scenic rating: 4

in Death Valley National Park

Wildrose is set on the road that heads out to the primitive country of the awesome Panamint Range, eventually coming within range of Telescope Peak, the highest point in Death Valley National Park (11,049 feet). The elevation at the camp is 4,100 feet.

Campsites, facilities: There are 23 sites for tents or RVs up to 25 feet (no hookups). Picnic tables and fire rings are provided. Drinking water (April through November only) and pit toilets are available. Campfires are not permitted during the summer. Leashed pets are permitted at campsites only.

Reservations, fees: No reservations are accepted and there is no camping fee; however, there is a $20 park entrance fee per vehicle that is valid for seven days. Open year-round.

Directions: From Stovepipe Wells Village, drive south on Highway 190 for eight miles to Emigrant Canyon Road (just past the Emigrant rest area). Turn left (east) on Emigrant

Canyon Road and drive 22 miles to the campground entrance on the left.

Contact: Death Valley National Park, 760/786-3200, fax 760/786-3283, www.nps.gov/deva.

8 THORNDIKE
🏃 🐕 ⛺

Scenic rating: 4

in Death Valley National Park

This is one of Death Valley National Park's little-known camps. It is set in the high country at 7,500 feet elevation. It's free, of course. Otherwise the park service would have to actually send somebody out to tend to the place. Nearby are century-old charcoal kilns that were built by Chinese laborers and tended by Shoshone workers. The trailhead that serves Telescope Peak (11,049 feet), the highest point in Death Valley, can be found in nearby Mahogany Flat.

Campsites, facilities: This backcountry campground is accessible only by foot or high-clearance vehicle; it has six sites for tents. Picnic tables and fire rings are provided. Pit toilets are available. No drinking water is available. Campfires are not permitted in the summer. Garbage must be packed out. Leashed pets are permitted at campsites only.

Reservations, fees: No reservations are accepted and there is no camping fee; however, there is a $20 park entrance fee per vehicle that is valid for seven days. Open March through November.

Directions: In Death Valley at Stovepipe Wells Village, drive south on Highway 190 for eight miles to Emigrant Canyon Road (just past the Emigrant rest area). Turn left (east) on Emigrant Canyon Road and drive 21 miles to Wildrose Canyon Road. Turn left and drive nine miles to the camp. (The road becomes extremely rough; high-clearance vehicle is required.)

Contact: Death Valley National Park,

760/786-3200, fax 760/786-3283, www.nps.gov/deva.

9 MAHOGANY FLAT FOUR-WHEEL DRIVE
🏃 🐕 ⛺

Scenic rating: 5

in Death Valley National Park

This is one of two primitive, hard-to-reach camps (the other is Thorndike) set in the Panamint Range high country. It is one of the few shaded camps, offering beautiful piñon pines and junipers. What makes it popular, however, is the trail to Telescope Peak leading out from camp. Only the ambitious and well conditioned should attempt the climb, a seven-mile trip one-way with breathtaking (literally) views of both Panamint Valley and Death Valley. The elevation at the campground is 8,200 feet and Telescope Peak tops out at 11,049 feet, which translates to a climb of 2,849 feet.

Campsites, facilities: There are 10 sites for tents only. Picnic tables and fire rings are provided. Pit toilets are available. No drinking water is available. Campfires are not permitted during the summer. Garbage must be packed out. The campground is accessible only by foot or high-clearance four-wheel-drive vehicle. Leashed pets are permitted at campsites only.

Reservations, fees: No reservations are accepted and there is no camping fee; however, there is a $20 park entrance fee per vehicle that is valid for seven days. Open March through November, weather permitting.

Directions: From Stovepipe Wells Village, drive south on Highway 190 for eight miles to Emigrant Canyon Road (just past the Emigrant rest area). Turn left (east) on Emigrant Canyon Road and drive 21 miles to Wildrose Canyon Road. Turn left and drive nine miles (passing Thorndike campground) to the end of the road and the camp.

Contact: Death Valley National Park,

CAMPING

760/786-3200, fax 760/786-3283, www. nps.gov/deva.

10 TECOPA HOT SPRINGS PARK
🌀 🏕 🚐 ⛺

Scenic rating: 3

north of Tecopa

This Inyo County campground is out there in no-man's land, and if it weren't for the hot springs and the good rockhounding, all you'd see around here would be a few skeletons. Regardless, it's quite an attraction in the winter, when the warm climate is a plus and the nearby mineral baths are worth taking a dunk in. Rockhounds will enjoy looking for amethysts, opals, and petrified wood in the nearby areas. The elevation is 1,500 feet. Nobody gets here by accident.

Campsites, facilities: There are 250 sites for tents or RVs of any length (with partial hookups of 30 amps). Some sites are pull-through. Picnic tables and fire grills are provided. Restrooms with flush toilets and showers and a dump station are available. There is no drinking water. Groceries and propane gas are available within 10 miles. Leashed pets are permitted.

Reservations, fees: Reservations are accepted. Sites are $14–17 per vehicle per night. Weekly and monthly rates are available. Open year-round.

Directions: From Baker, drive north on Highway 127 for 58 miles to a county road signed "Tecopa Hot Springs" (south of the junction of Highway 178 and Highway 127). Turn right (east) and drive five miles to the park and campground entrance.

Contact: Tecopa Hot Springs Park, 760/852-4481.

11 RED ROCK CANYON STATE PARK
🚶 🐴 ♿ 🚐 ⛺

Scenic rating: 8

near Mojave

This unique state park is one of the prettiest spots in the region year-round. What makes it worthwhile in any season is the chance to see wondrous geologic formations, most of them tinted red. The park also has paleontology sites, as well as remnants of some 1890s-era mining operations. A great, easy hike is the two-mile walk to Red Cliffs Natural Preserve, where there are awesome 300-foot cliffs and columns, painted red by the iron in the soil. Part of this area is closed February through June to protect nesting raptors. For those who don't hike, a must is driving up Jawbone Canyon Road to see Jawbone and Last Chance Canyons. Hikers have it better. The park also has excellent wildflower blooms March through May. A primitive OHV trail also is available; check regulations. The elevation is 2,600 feet.

Campsites, facilities: There are 50 sites for tents or RVs up to 30 feet (no hookups). Picnic tables and fire grills are provided. Drinking water, pit toilets, dump station, picnic area, seasonal exhibits, seasonal campfire program, and a seasonal nature trail are available. In spring and fall, nature walks led by rangers are available. Some facilities are wheelchair-accessible. Leashed pets are permitted in the campground only.

Reservations, fees: Reservations are not accepted. Sites are $12 per night, and $5 for each additional vehicle. Open year-round.

Directions: Drive on Highway 14 to the town of Mojave (50 miles east of the Los Angeles Basin area). Continue northeast on Highway 14 for 25 miles to the park entrance on the left.

Contact: Red Rock Canyon State Park, 661/320-4001, www.parks.ca.gov.

12 BRITE VALLEY AQUATIC RECREATION AREA
🚶 🛶 🚤 ⛵ 🐎 🎣 🚐 ⛺

Scenic rating: 7

at Brite Lake

Brite Valley Lake is a speck of a water hole (90 acres) on the northern flank of the Tehachapi Mountains in Kern County, at an elevation of 4,000 feet. No gas motors are permitted on the lake, so it's perfect for canoes, kayaks, or inflatables. No swimming is permitted. Use is moderate, primarily by picnickers and anglers. The lake is stocked with trout in the spring and catfish in the summer. Other species include bluegill. A golf course is nearby.

Campsites, facilities: There are 12 sites with partial hookups (20 amps) for RVs of any length and a tent camping area. Picnic tables and fire grills are provided. Drinking water, restroom with flush toilets and showers, dump station, playground, picnic pavilions (available by reservation), and fish-cleaning station are available. Supplies are available about eight miles away in Tehachapi. Leashed pets are permitted.

Reservations, fees: Reservations are not accepted. Sites are $15–30 per night for each vehicle. Boat launching is $5 per day. Open year-round.

Directions: From Bakersfield, drive east on Highway 58 for 40 miles toward the town of Tehachapi. Take the Highway 202 exit and drive three miles west to Banducci Road. Turn left and drive for about one mile to the park on the right.

Contact: Tehachapi Valley Recreation and Parks District, 661/822-3228, fax 661/823-8529.

13 INDIAN HILL RANCH AND RV PARK
🚶 🛶 🐎 🚐 ⛺

Scenic rating: 7

near Tehachapi

This is a unique park with two seasonal ponds stocked with largemouth bass and catfish. Crappie and bluegill are other fish species. The campground is open year-round and offers spacious, private sites with oak trees and a view of Brite Valley. A bonus is the hiking trails in the park. The elevation is 5,000 feet. Although this area is known for being windy, this campground is somewhat sheltered from the wind.

Campsites, facilities: There are 46 sites for RVs, including 37 sites with full hookups; nearly half are pull-through. Tents are allowed only in sites without hookups. Picnic tables and fire pits are provided. Restroom with flush toilets and showers (seasonal), dump station, coin laundry, Wi-Fi, propane, and two stocked fishing ponds are available. Small leashed pets are permitted, with certain restrictions.

Reservations, fees: Reservations are accepted. Sites are $20–40 per night. Monthly and group rates available. No credit cards accepted. Open year-round, with some sites closed November through mid-May.

Directions: Drive on Highway 58 to Tehachapi and Exit 148 for Tehachapi/Highway 202. Take that exit to Tucker Road. Turn right and drive south one mile to Highway 202/Valley Boulevard. Turn right (west) and drive four miles to Banducci Road. Turn left and drive 0.75 mile to Arosa Road. Turn left and drive 1.7 miles to the park at 18061 Arosa Road.

Contact: Indian Hill Ranch and RV Park, 661/822-6613, www.indianhillranch.com.

14 TEHACHAPI MOUNTAIN PARK

🏃 🏕 ♿ 🚐 ⛺

Scenic rating: 6

southwest of Tehachapi

This county park is overlooked by most out-of-towners. It is a pretty spot covering 5,000 acres, set on the slopes of the Tehachapi Mountains, with elevations in the park ranging from 5,500 to 7,000 feet. The roads to the campgrounds are steep, but the sites are flat. Trails for hikers and equestrians are available, but no horses are allowed at the campground. An interpretive trail, Nuooah Nature Trail, is available. This park is popular not only in spring, but also in winter, with the elevations sometimes high enough to get snow (chains often required for access). The park lies eight miles southwest of the town of Tehachapi on the southern side of Highway 58 between Mojave and Bakersfield. Woody's Peak, at almost 8,000 feet, overlooks the park from its dominion in the Tehachapi Mountains, the dividing line between the San Joaquin Valley and the Los Angeles Basin.

Campsites, facilities: There are 61 sites for tents or RVs of any length (no hookups), a group campsite for up to 40 people, a group campsite for up to 150 people, and group lodging with 10 cabins for a minimum of 40 people. Picnic tables and fire grills are provided. Drinking water (natural spring) and chemical toilets are available. Some facilities are wheelchair-accessible. Leashed pets are permitted.

Reservations, fees: Reservations are not accepted for individual sites, but are required for the group sites and group cabins at 661/868-7002. Sites are $14 per night per vehicle, $60–275 per night for the group site, and $2 per pet per night. Open year-round, weather permitting.

Directions: In Tehachapi, take Tehachapi Boulevard to the Cury Street exit. Take that exit south and drive about three miles to Highline Road. Turn right on Highline Road and drive two miles to Water Canyon Road. Turn left on Water Canyon Road and drive three miles to the park.

Contact: Kern County Parks Department info line, 661/868-7000, www.co.kern.ca.us/parks/index.htm.

15 OWL CANYON

🏃 🐕 🚐 ⛺

Scenic rating: 3

near Barstow

The primary attraction of Owl Canyon camp is that the surrounding desert is sprinkled with exposed fossils of ancient animals. Guess they couldn't find any water. Well, if people try hiking here without a full canteen, there may soon be some human skeletons out here, too. Actually, rangers say that the general public is unlikely to spot fossils here because it takes some basic scientific knowledge to identify them. The sparse BLM land out here is kind of like an ugly dog you learn to love: After a while, when you look closely, you learn it has a heart of gold. This region is best visited in the spring and fall, of course, when hiking allows a fresh, new look at what may appear to some as a wasteland. The beauty is in the detail of it—tiny critters and tiny flowers seen against the unfenced vastness, with occasional fossils yet to be discovered. The elevation is 2,600 feet.

Campsites, facilities: There are 31 sites for tents or RVs of any length (no hookups). Picnic tables and fire grills are provided. Vault toilets are available. There is no drinking water. Leashed pets are permitted.

Reservations, fees: Reservations are not accepted. Sites are $6 per night. Open year-round.

Directions: Drive on I-15 to Barstow to the exit for 1st Street. Take that exit and drive north on 1st Street (crossing the Mojave River Bridge) for 0.75 mile to Irwin Road. Turn left and drive eight miles to Fossil Bed Road. Turn left and drive two miles to the campground on the right.

Contact: Bureau of Land Management, Barstow Field Office, 760/252-6000, fax 760/252-6099.

16 CALICO GHOST TOWN REGIONAL PARK

Scenic rating: 4

near Barstow

Let me tell you about this ghost town: There are probably more people here now than there have ever been. In the 1880s and 1890s it was a booming silver mine town, and there are still remnants of that. Alas, it now has lots of restaurants and shops. Recreation options include riding on a narrow-gauge railroad, touring what was once the largest silver mine in California, and watching an old-style melodrama with villains and heroes. This is a 480-acre park with self-guided tours, hiking trails, gold panning, summer entertainment, and museum, with festivals held throughout the year. Whatever you do, don't take any artifacts you may come across, such as an old nail, a jar, or anything; you will be doomed with years of bad luck. No foolin'. A park representative told the story of a man from the East Coast who nabbed a beautiful rock on his visit. He then was plagued with years of bad luck, including broken bones, disappointment in his love life, and several family deaths. In desperation, he flew back to California and returned the rock to its rightful place.

Campsites, facilities: There are 253 sites for tents and RVs up to 45 feet; 104 sites have full or partial hookups (20, 30, and 50 amps) and some sites are pull-through. There are also three group camping areas, six cabins, and a bunkhouse. Fire pits are provided. Restrooms with flush toilets and showers, drinking water, and three dump stations are available. Pay phone, restaurants, and shops are on-site. Groceries, propane gas, and laundry facilities are 10 miles away. Some facilities are wheelchair-accessible. Leashed pets are permitted.

Reservations, fees: Reservations are accepted at 800/TO-CALICO (800/862-2542) 8 A.M.–3 P.M. ($2 reservation fee). Sites are $20–25 per night, $1 per pet per night. Some credit cards accepted. Open year-round.

Directions: From Barstow, drive northeast on I-15 for seven miles to the exit for Ghost Town Road. Take that exit and drive north on Ghost Town Road for three miles to the park on the left.

Contact: Calico Ghost Town Regional Park, San Bernardino County, 760/254-2122, fax 760/254-2047, www.calicotown.com.

17 BARSTOW CALICO KOA

Scenic rating: 3

near Barstow

Don't blame me if you end up way out here. Actually, for vacationers making the long-distance grind of a drive on I-15, this KOA can seem like the promised land. It has received awards for its cleanliness, and a nightly quiet time ensures that you have a chance to get rested. Vegetation screening between sites enhance privacy. But hey, as long as you're here, you might as well take a side trip to Calico Ghost Town, about three miles to the northeast at the foot of the Calico Mountains. A unique side trip is the Calico Early Man Site, about five miles to the north; tours are available. Primitive stone tools are believed to have been discovered here in 1942. Rockhounding, hiking, and an outlet mall are other nearby options. The elevation is 1,900 feet.

Campsites, facilities: There are 78 sites with full or partial hookups (30 and 50 amps) for tents or RVs of any length; many are pull-through. Picnic tables and fire grills are provided. Drinking water, restrooms with flush toilets and showers, dump station, modem access, playground, heated swimming pool, recreation room, convenience store, propane gas, ice, and coin laundry are available. Some facilities are wheelchair-accessible. Leashed pets are permitted.

Reservations, fees: Reservations are accepted at 800/KOA-0059 (800/562-0059). Sites are $26–46 per night, $3.50 per person per night for more than two people. Some credit cards accepted. Open year-round.

Directions: From Barstow, drive northeast on I-15 for seven miles to the exit for Ghost Town Road. Take that exit and drive left under the freeway to a frontage road at the Shell gas station. Turn left at the frontage road and drive 0.25 mile to the campground on the right.

Contact: Barstow Calico KOA, 760/254-2311, fax 760/254-2247, www.koa.com.

18 AFTON CANYON
🏃 🐴 🚙 ⛺

Scenic rating: 6

near Barstow in the East Mojave National Scenic Area

This camp is set at 1,400 feet elevation in a desert riparian habitat along the Mojave River. This is one of several Bureau of Land Management tracts near the Mojave National Preserve. Side-trip options include the Rainbow Basin Natural Area (about an hour's drive), Soda Springs, and the Calico Early Man Site. Remember, rivers in the desert are not like rivers in cooler climates. There are no fish worth eating.

Campsites, facilities: There are 22 sites for tents or RVs up to 30 feet (no hookups). Picnic tables and fire rings are provided. Vault toilets are available. Drinking water is available intermittently, so bring your own water. Leashed pets are permitted.

Reservations, fees: Reservations are not accepted. Sites are $6 per night. Open year-round.

Directions: From Barstow, drive east on I-15 for 37 miles to Afton Road. Turn right (south) and drive three miles to the campground. Note: Four-wheel-drive or high-clearance vehicles are recommended since the access road can be rough and have washouts.

Contact: Bureau of Land Management, Barstow Field Office, 760/252-6000, fax 760/252-6099.

19 PROVIDENCE MOUNTAINS STATE RECREATION AREA
🏃 🐴 🚙 ⛺

Scenic rating: 8

near Mitchell Caverns

This remote desert park, set at 4,300 feet elevation, offers guided tours of Mitchell Caverns ($2–4 tour fee, discounts available). These tours are available daily from early September through Memorial Day weekend, and on weekends from Memorial Day through early September. It's a good idea to make a reservation for the tour at 760/928-2586. The cavern tours are the reason most people visit and camp at this park. The caverns are classic limestone formations. There are additional recreational opportunities. From the campground Nina Mora Overlook Trail is a short (0.25-mile) walk to a lookout of the Marble Mountains and the valley below. Another short hike with a great view is the steep, one-mile hike (one-way) on Crystal Springs Trail, the best of the bunch. Another hike is Mary Beale, an interpretive trail accessible from the visitors center, a one-mile loop.

Campsites, facilities: There are six sites for tents or RVs up to 31 feet (no hookups). Picnic tables and fire grills are provided. Drinking water and flush toilets are available. A pay phone is nearby. Leashed pets are permitted in the campground only.

Reservations, fees: Reservations are not accepted. Sites are $12 per night, $5 per night for each additional vehicle. Open year-round.

Directions: Drive on I-40 to Essex Road (near Essex, 116 miles east of Barstow). Take that road and drive north on Essex Road for 16 miles to the park at road's end.

Contact: Providence Mountains State Recreation Area, 760/928-2586; Mojave Desert Information Center, 661/942-0662, fax 661/940-7327, www.parks.ca.gov.

20 MID HILLS
🏃 🐴 🚐 ⛺

Scenic rating: 4

in the Mojave National Preserve

This is a primitive campground set among the junipers and piñon trees in a mountainous area at 5,600 feet elevation. It is one of two little-known camps in the vast desert that is now managed by the National Park Service. About two-thirds of the campsites were burned in the 2005 Hackberry Fire; most of the piñon and juniper trees burned as well. There is an eight-mile one-way trail that starts across from the entrance to Mid Hills and is routed down to the Hole-in-the-Wall Campground. It a pleasant walk in spring and fall.

Campsites, facilities: There are 26 sites for tents or RVs up to 22 feet (no hookups). Picnic tables and fire grills are provided. Drinking water and vault toilets are available. Leashed pets are permitted.

Reservations, fees: Reservations are not accepted. Sites are $12 per night. Open year-round.

Directions: Drive on I-40 to Essex Road (near Essex, 116 miles east of Barstow). Take that exit and drive north on Essex Road for 10 miles to Black Canyon Road. Turn north and drive nine miles (at Hole-in-the-Wall campground, the road becomes dirt) and continue seven miles to Wild Horse Canyon Road. Turn left and drive two miles (rough, dirt road) to the campground on the right.

Contact: Mojave National Preserve, 760/252-

6100, fax 760/252-6174, www.nps.gov/moja.

21 HOLE-IN-THE-WALL (AND BLACK CANYON GROUP AND HORSE CAMP)
🏃 🐴 🚐 ⛺

Scenic rating: 6

in the Mojave National Preserve

This is the largest and best-known of the camps in the vast Mojave National Preserve. There are three camps: a family camp across the street from a group camp and an equestrian camp. All are set at 4,400 feet elevation. An interesting side trip is to the Mitchell Caverns in the nearby Providence Mountains State Recreation Area.

Campsites, facilities: There are 35 sites for tents or RVs of any length (no hookups), one group site for up to 50 people, and an equestrian camp. Picnic tables and fire grills are provided. Drinking water, vault toilets, and a dump station are available. Leashed pets are permitted.

Reservations, fees: Reservations are not accepted. Sites are $12 per night. Make reservations for group camp and horse camp at 760/928-2572; $25 per night, including horse corral if needed. Open year-round.

Directions: Drive on I-40 to Essex Road (near Essex, 116 miles east of Barstow). Take that exit and drive north on Essex Road for 10 miles to Black Canyon Road. Turn north and drive nine miles to the campgrounds.

Contact: Mojave National Preserve, 760/252-6100, fax 760/252-6174, www.nps.gov/moja.

22 RAINBO BEACH RESORT

Scenic rating: 6

on the Colorado River

The big bonus here is the full marina, making this resort on the Colorado River the headquarters for boaters and water-skiers. And headquarters it is, with tons of happy folks who are extremely well lubed, both inside and out. This resort boasts 800 feet of river frontage. A 70-site mobile home park is adjacent to the RV park. (For boating details, see the *Needles Marina Park* listing in this chapter.)

Campsites, facilities: There are 64 sites with full hookups (30 and 50 amps) for RVs. Some sites are pull-through. Picnic tables are provided. Restrooms with showers, coin laundry, heated swimming pool, spa, recreation room, and a restaurant are available. A boat dock is nearby. Leashed pets are permitted.

Reservations, fees: Reservations are accepted. Sites are $25–28 per night. Seasonal rates available. Some credit cards accepted. Open year-round.

Directions: Drive on I-40 to Needles and River Road. Turn north on River Road and drive 1.5 miles to the resort on the right.

Contact: Rainbo Beach Resort, 760/326-3101, fax 760/326-5085.

23 NEEDLES MARINA PARK

Scenic rating: 6

on the Colorado River

Bring your suntan lotion and a beach towel. This section of the Colorado River is a big tourist spot where the body oil and beer can flow faster than the river. There are a ton of hot bodies and hot boats, and waterskiing dominates the adjacent calm-water section of the Colorado River. However, note that upstream of the Needles-area put-in is the prime area for waterskiing. Downstream is the chance for canoeing or kayaking. Meanwhile, there's also an 18-hole golf course adjacent to the camp, but most folks head for the river. Compared to the surrounding desert, this park is almost a golden paradise. A mobile home park is adjacent to the RV park.

Campsites, facilities: There are 158 sites with full hookups (30 and 50 amps) for tents or RVs, and six cabins. Some sites are pull-through. Picnic tables are provided. Restrooms with flush toilets and showers, drinking water, heated pool, spa, recreation room, Wi-Fi, modem access, playground, picnic area, boat ramp, boat slips, store, gas, and laundry facilities are available. Leashed pets are permitted.

Reservations, fees: Reservations are accepted. Sites are $34–36 per night, $4.50 per night for air conditioning, $5 per pet per night. Some credit cards accepted. Open year-round.

Directions: Drive on I-40 to Needles and the exit for J Street. Take that exit and drive to Broadway. Turn left on Broadway and drive 0.75 mile to Needles Highway. Turn right (north) on Needles Highway and drive 0.5 mile to the park on the left.

Contact: Needles Marina Park, 760/326-2197, fax 760/326-4125, www.needlesmarinapark. com.

24 NEEDLES KOA

Scenic rating: 2

near the Colorado River

At least you've got the Needles KOA out here, complete with swimming pool, where you can get a new start. Side trips include venturing to the nearby Colorado River or heading north to Lake Mead. Of course, you could always go to Las Vegas. Nah.

Campsites, facilities: There are 93 pull-through sites with full hookups (30 and 50 amps), and 18 pull-through sites with partial hookups (30 and 50 amps) for tents or RVs of any length. Five cabins are also available. Restrooms with flush toilets and showers, drinking water, recreation room, swimming pool, playground, store, snack bar, propane gas, and coin laundry are available. Some facilities are wheelchair-accessible. Leashed pets are permitted.

Reservations, fees: Reservations are accepted at 800/562-3407. Sites are $22–32 per night, $2 per person per night for more than two people. Credit cards accepted. Open year-round.

Directions: Drive on I-40 to Needles and the exit for West Broadway. Take that exit to Needles Highway. Turn northwest on Needles Highway and drive 0.75 mile to National Old Trails Highway. Turn left and drive one mile to the park on the right (5400 National Old Trails Highway).

Contact: Needles KOA, 760/326-4207, fax 760/326-6329, www.koa.com.

25 MOABI REGIONAL PARK

🏊 🎣 🚤 🐕 ♿ 🚐 ⛺

Scenic rating: 7

on the Colorado River

BEST (

Campsites are situated in the main area of the park along 2.5 miles of shoreline peninsula. The park features 24 group areas. The adjacent Colorado River provides the main attraction, the only thing liquid around these parts that isn't contained in a can or bottle. The natural response when you see it is to jump in the water, and everybody does so, with or without a boat. You'll see lots of wild and crazy types having the times of their lives on the water. The boating season is a long one here, courtesy of that desert climate. Fishing is good for catfish, smallmouth bass, bluegill, striped bass, and sometimes crappie.

Campsites, facilities: There is a large grassy area for tents and more than 600 sites for RVs or tents—155 with full or partial hookups (20, 30, and 50 amps), and a few are pull-through.

There are also 24 group camping areas. Picnic tables and fire grills are provided at most sites. Restrooms with flush toilets and showers, coin laundry, store, ice, dump station, covered picnic area, marina, bait, and boat ramp are available. Volleyball, basketball, horseshoes, and putting green are also available. An 18-hole golf course is nearby. Some facilities are wheelchair-accessible. Leashed pets are permitted.

Reservations, fees: Reservations are accepted. Sites are $15–35 per night per vehicle, $1 per pet per night. Long-term rates available in the winter, with limit of five months. Some credit cards accepted. Open year-round.

Directions: From Needles, drive east on I-40 for 11 miles to Park Moabi Road. Turn left on Park Moabi Road and continue 0.5 mile to the park entrance at the end of the road.

Contact: Moabi Regional Park Marina, 760/326-3831, fax 760/326-3272; San Bernardino County, 760/326-4777, www.co.san-bernardino.ca.us/parks/moabi.htm.

26 KINGS

🐕 🚐 ⛺

Scenic rating: 5

near Piru Creek in Los Padres National Forest

The Hungry Valley State Vehicular Recreation Area is just five miles to the east. Figure it out: Right, this is a primitive but well-placed camp for four-wheel-drive and off-highway vehicles. The camp is near Piru Creek, off a short spur road, so it feels remote yet is close to one of California's top off-road areas.

Campsites, facilities: There are seven sites for tents or RVs up to 16 feet (no hookups). Picnic tables and fire grills are provided. Vault toilets are available. No drinking water is available. Garbage must be packed out. Leashed pets are permitted.

Reservations, fees: No reservations are accepted and there is no camping fee. An Adventure

Pass ($30 annual fee or $5 daily fee) per parked vehicle is required. Open year-round.

Directions: Drive on I-5 to south of Gorman and the Gorman–Hungry Valley Road exit (the northern exit for the Hungry Valley Recreation Area). Take that exit and turn south on Hungry Valley Road (Forest Road 8N01) and drive six miles to Gold Hill Road (Forest Road 8N01). Turn right and drive six miles to Forest Road 18N01A. Turn left and drive 0.75 mile to the campground.

Contact: Los Padres National Forest, Mount Piños Ranger District, 661/245-3731, fax 661/245-1526.

27 LOS ALAMOS
🚶 🏊 🛶 🎣 🐕 ♿ 🚐 ⛰️

Scenic rating: 4

near Pyramid Lake in Angeles National Forest

BEST (

Los Alamos is set at an elevation of 2,600 feet near the southern border of the Hungry Valley State Vehicular Recreation Area, and about 2.5 miles north of Pyramid Lake. Pyramid Lake is a big lake, covering 1,300 acres with 20 miles of shoreline, and is extremely popular for waterskiing and fast boating (35 mph speed limit), as well as for sailboarding (best at the northern launch point), fishing (best in the spring and early summer and in the fall for striped bass), and swimming. A lifeguard is on duty at the boat launch area during the summer season.

Campsites, facilities: There are 93 sites and three group sites for tents or RVs up to 40 feet (no hookups) that can accommodate up to 25 people each. Picnic tables and fire pits are provided. Drinking water and flush toilets are available. A boat ramp is at the Emigrant Landing Picnic Area. Some facilities are wheelchair-accessible. Leashed pets are permitted.

Reservations, fees: Reservations are not accepted for individual sites, but are required for group sites at 661/248-6725. Sites are $14 per night, $7 per night per each additional

vehicle, $65 per night for a group site. Open year-round.

Directions: Drive on I-5 to eight miles south of Gorman and the Smokey Bear Road exit. Take the Smokey Bear Road exit and drive west about three-quarters of a mile and follow the signs to the campground.

Contact: Recreation Resource Management, 661/248-6725; National Forest, Santa Clara/Mojave Rivers Ranger District, 661/296-9710, fax 661/296-5847.

28 DUTCHMAN FLAT
🚶 🐕 ⛰️

Scenic rating: 6

on Alamo Mountain in Los Padres National Forest

Dutchman is set at 6,800 feet elevation. These spots are best known by four-wheel-drive enthusiasts rumbling around the area. The big attraction here is access to Miller Jeep Trail, a gnarly black-diamond route that can bend metal and alter minds. This camp also provides an alternative to the Hungry Valley State Vehicular Recreation Area to the nearby northeast.

Campsites, facilities: There are eight primitive sites. Picnic tables and fire grills are provided. Pit toilets are available. No drinking water is available. Garbage must be packed out. Leashed pets are permitted.

Reservations, fees: No reservations are accepted and there is no camping fee. An Adventure Pass ($30 annual fee or $5 daily pass) per parked vehicle is required. Open early May through October, weather permitting.

Directions: Drive on I-5 to south of Gorman and the Gorman–Hungry Valley Road exit (the northern exit for the Hungry Valley Recreation Area). Take that exit and turn south on Hungry Valley Road (Forest Road 8N01) and drive six miles to Gold Hill Road (Forest Road 8N01). Turn right and drive 13 miles to Twin Pines campground. To reach Dutch-

man, at Twin Pines campground, turn right at Forest Road 7N01 and drive three miles to the campground.
Contact: Los Padres National Forest, Mount Piños Ranger District, 661/245-3731, fax 661/245-1526.

29 HALF MOON

Scenic rating: 7

near Piru Creek in Los Padres National Forest

Half Moon is a primitive camp set along Piru Creek at 4,700 feet elevation. Adjacent to camp, Forest Road 7N13 follows the creek for a few miles, then dead-ends at a trailhead that continues along more remote stretches of this little stream. Hikers should also consider the trail to nearby Thorn Point for a beautiful lookout.

Campsites, facilities: There are 10 sites for tents or RVs up to 22 feet (no hookups). Picnic tables and fire grills are provided. Pit toilets are available. No drinking water is available. Garbage must be packed out. Leashed pets are permitted.

Reservations, fees: No reservations are accepted and there is no camping fee. An Adventure Pass ($30 annual fee or $5 daily pas) per parked vehicle is required. Open seasonally, weather permitting.

Directions: Drive on I-5 to just south of Lebec and the Frazier Park exit. Take that exit and drive west on Frazier Mountain Road to the town of Lake of the Woods and Lockwood Valley Road. Turn left on Lockwood Valley Road and drive about 12 miles to Grade Valley Road (Forest Road 7N03). Turn left and drive 11 miles to the campground on the left. High-clearance or four-wheel-drive vehicles are recommended; access requires crossing a creek in which the current can be fairly fast and high, especially in the spring.
Contact: Los Padres National Forest, Mount

Piños Ranger District, 661/245-3731, fax 661/245-1526.

30 SAWMILL

Scenic rating: 7

on the Pacific Crest Trail in Angeles National Forest

This is a classic hikers trailhead camp. It is set at 5,200 feet elevation, right on the Pacific Crest Trail and just one mile from the junction with Burnt Peak Canyon Trail. For a good day hike, head southeast on the Pacific Crest Trail for one mile to Burnt Peak Canyon Trail, turn right (southwest), and hike just over a mile to Burnt Peak, at 5,788 feet elevation. Note that this camp is inaccessible after the first snow. Nearby Upper Shake provides an alternative.

Campsites, facilities: There are eight sites for tents or RVs up to 16 feet (no hookups). Note that RVs are not recommended. Picnic tables and fire pits are provided. Vault toilets are available. No drinking water is available. Garbage must be packed out. Leashed pets are permitted.

Reservations, fees: No reservations are accepted and there is no camping fee. An Adventure Pass ($30 annual fee or $5 daily pass) per parked vehicle is required. Open May through October, weather permitting.

Directions: Drive on I-5 to the Tehachapis near the small town of Castaic and Lake Hughes Road. Turn northeast on Lake Hughes Road and drive 27 miles to the town of Lake Hughes and Pine Canyon Road/County Road N2. Turn left on Pine Canyon Road and drive 10 miles to Bushnell Summit Road. Turn left and drive two miles to the campground on the left.
Contact: Angeles National Forest, Santa Clara/Mojave Rivers Ranger District, 661/296-9710, fax 661/296-5847.

CAMPING

31 UPPER SHAKE

Scenic rating: 7

on the Pacific Crest Trail in Angeles National Forest

Upper Shake, like nearby Sawmill, is right on the Pacific Crest Trail. The elevation is 4,400 feet. Hikers who plan on heading to Burnt Peak are better off departing from Sawmill (less than two miles to the west). This camp is used primarily as a jump-off point for those heading east on the PCT; Lake Hughes is the nearest destination, less than four miles away, and a mile after that is Lake Elizabeth. The camp is inaccessible after the first snow.

Campsites, facilities: There are 18 sites for tents or RVs up to 22 feet (no hookups). Picnic tables and fire pits are provided. Vault toilets are available. No drinking water is available. Garbage must be packed out. Leashed pets are permitted.

Reservations, fees: No reservations are accepted and there is no camping fee. An Adventure Pass ($30 annual fee or $5 daily pass) per parked vehicle is required. Open May through October, weather permitting.

Directions: Drive on I-5 to the Tehachapis near the small town of Castaic and Lake Hughes Road. Turn northeast on Lake Hughes Road and drive 27 miles to the town of Lake Hughes and Pine Canyon Road/County Road N2. Turn left on Pine Canyon Road and drive about 5.5 miles to the entrance road on the left.

Contact: Angeles National Forest, Santa Clara/Mojave Rivers Ranger District, 661/296-9710, fax 661/296-5847.

32 COTTONWOOD

Scenic rating: 5

near the Warm Springs Mountain Lookout in Angeles National Forest

Cottonwood Camp is set at 2,680 feet elevation in remote Angeles National Forest along a small stream. The camp is on the north flank of Warm Springs Mountain. A great side trip is to the Warm Springs Mountain Lookout (4,023 feet), about a five-mile drive. Drive south on Forest Road 7N09 for three miles, turn right (west) on Forest Road 6N32, and drive for 1.5 miles to Forest Road 7N13. Turn left (south) and drive a mile to the summit.

Campsites, facilities: There are 22 sites for tents or RVs up to 22 feet (no hookups). Picnic tables and fire pits are provided. Vault toilets are available. No drinking water is available. Garbage must be packed out. Supplies are less than four miles away in the town of Lake Hughes. Leashed pets are permitted.

Reservations, fees: No reservations are accepted and there is no camping fee. An Adventure Pass ($30 annual fee or $5 daily pass) per parked vehicle is required. Open year-round, weather permitting.

Directions: Drive on I-5 to the Tehachapis near the small town of Castaic and Lake Hughes Road. Turn northeast on Lake Hughes Road and drive 27 miles to the campground on the right.

Contact: Angeles National Forest, Santa Clara/Mojave Rivers Ranger District, 661/296-9710, fax 661/296-5847.

33 SADDLEBACK BUTTE STATE PARK

🏃 🏕 ᚛ 🚙 ⛰

Scenic rating: 8

near Lancaster

This 3,000-acre park was originally established to preserve ancient Joshua trees. In fact, it used to be called Joshua Tree State Park, but folks kept getting it confused with Joshua Tree National Park, so it was renamed. The terrain is sparsely vegetated and desertlike, with excellent hiking trails up the nearby buttes. The best hike is Saddleback Loop, a five-mile trip that features a 1,000-foot climb to Saddleback Summit at 3,651 feet. On rare clear days, there are fantastic views in all directions, including the Antelope Valley California Poppy Preserve, the surrounding mountains, and the Mojave Desert. On the typical hazy day, the poppy preserve might as well be on the moon; you can't even come close to seeing it. The elevation is 2,700 feet.

Campsites, facilities: There are 30 sites for tents or RVs up to 30 feet (no hookups). A group camp is available for up to 30 people. Picnic tables, shade ramadas, and fire grills are provided. Drinking water, flush toilets, and dump station are available. A visitors center is nearby. Some facilities are wheelchair-accessible. Leashed pets are permitted in the campground only.

Reservations, fees: Reservations are not accepted for individual sites, but the group camp may be reserved at 800/444-PARK (800/444-7275) or www.reserveamerica.com ($7.50 reservation fee). Sites are $12 per night, $5 per night for each additional vehicle, $66 per night for the group site. Open year-round.

Directions: Drive north on Highway 14 to Lancaster and the exit for Avenue J. Take that exit and drive east on Avenue J for 17 miles to the park entrance on the right.

Or drive south on Highway 14 to Lancaster to the exit for 20th Street west. Take that exit, turn left, and drive to Avenue J. Turn east

on Avenue J and drive 17 miles to the park entrance on the right.

Contact: Saddleback Butte State Park, Mojave Desert Information Center, 661/942-0662, fax 661/940-7327, www.parks.ca.gov.

34 DESERT WILLOW RV PARK

🏊 🏕 ᚛ 🚙

Scenic rating: 2

in Hesperia

This is an RV park for I-15 cruisers looking to make a stop. Silverwood Lake, a 1,000-acre recreation lake with fishing, boating, and water sports, is 18 miles to the south. The elevation is 3,200 feet.

Campsites, facilities: There are 176 sites with full hookups (30 and 50 amps) for RVs up to 70 feet; some sites are pull-through. No tents. Note that only 17 sites are available for overnight campers. Restrooms with showers, cable TV hookups, ice, coin laundry, propane gas, swimming pool, indoor spa, billiard room, exercise room, and library are on the premises. Some facilities are wheelchair-accessible. Leashed pets are permitted.

Reservations, fees: Reservations are accepted at 800/900-8114. Sites are $35 per night. Monthly rates available. Open year-round.

Directions: Drive on I-15 to Hesperia and Exit 143. Take that exit to Main Street. Turn west and drive to the park on the right (12624 Main Street West).

Contact: Desert Willow RV Park, 760/949-0377, fax 760/949-4334.

CAMPING

35 SHADY OASIS VICTORVILLE

Scenic rating: 3

near Victorville

Most long-distance trips on I-15 are gruel-ing endurance tests with drivers making the mistake of trying to get a decent night's sleep at a roadside rest stop. Why endure the torture, especially with Shady Oasis way out here, in Victorville of all places? Where the heck is Victorville? If you are exhausted and lucky enough to find the place, you won't be making any jokes about it. Note: There are about 50 permanent residents at this former KOA.

Campsites, facilities: There are 136 sites for tents or RVs of any length, many with full or partial hookups (50 amps) and some pull-through. There are also eight cabins. Picnic tables and fire grills are provided. Drinking water, restrooms with flush toilets and showers, recreation room, seasonal heated swimming pool, playground, modem access, convenience store, propane gas, and coin laundry are available. Some facilities are wheelchair-accessible. Leashed pets are permitted.

Reservations, fees: Reservations are accepted at 760/245-6867. Sites are $26–46 per night, $3 per person for more than two people, $1 per night for each additional vehicle. Some credit cards accepted. Open year-round.

Directions: Drive on I-15 to Victorville and Stoddard Wells Road (north of Victorville). Turn south on Stoddard Wells Road and drive a short distance to the campground (16530 Stoddard Wells Road).

Contact: Shady Oasis Victorville, 760/245-6867, fax 760/243-2108.

36 HESPERIA LAKE CAMPGROUND

Scenic rating: 5

in Hesperia

This is a slightly more rustic alternative to Desert Willow RV Park in Hesperia. There is a small lake/pond for recreational fishing and there is a small fishing fee, but no fishing license is required. Boating and swimming are not allowed, but youngsters usually get a kick out of feeding the ducks and geese that live at the pond.

Campsites, facilities: There are 52 sites with partial hookups (30 and 50 amps) for tents or RVs up to 40 feet. Picnic tables and fire pits are provided. Drinking water, restrooms with flush toilets and showers, a playground, and a fishing pond are available. Some facilities are wheelchair-accessible. Leashed pets are permitted.

Reservations, fees: Reservations are accepted at 800/521-6332. Sites are $35 per night, $2 per night per pet, $15 to fish at the pond. Some credit cards accepted. Open year-round.

Directions: Drive on I-15 to Hesperia and the exit for Main Street. Take that exit and drive east on Main Street for 9.5 miles (the road curves and becomes Arrowhead Lake Road) to the park on the left.

Contact: Hesperia Lake Campground, 760/244-5951 or 800/521-6332.

37 MOJAVE NARROWS REGIONAL PARK

Scenic rating: 7

on the Mojave River

Almost no one except the locals knows about this little county park. It is like an oasis in the Mojave Desert. There are actually two small lakes here: the larger Horseshoe Lake and Pelican Lake. No private boats are allowed and rental rowboats and pedal boats are available on weekends. Swimming and water/body contact are prohibited. It is set at 2,000 feet elevation and provides a few recreation options, including a pond stocked in season with trout and catfish, horseback-riding facilities, and equestrian trails. Hiking includes a wheelchair-accessible trail. The Mojave River level fluctuates here, almost disappearing in some years in summer and early fall. One of the big events of the year here, the Huck Finn Jubilee, is on Father's Day in June. Note: The gate closes each evening.

Campsites, facilities: There are 110 sites for tents or RVs of any length; seven pull-through, 42 with full hookups (15 and 30 amps). Fourteen group areas are also available. Picnic tables and barbecue grills are provided. Drinking water, restrooms with flush toilets and showers, dump station, snack bar, playground, picnic shelters, bait, boat rentals, horse rentals, and horseback-riding facilities are available. A store, propane gas, and coin laundry are available three miles from the campground. Leashed pets are permitted.

Reservations, fees: Reservations accepted for RVs and groups. Sites are $15–22 per night, $1 per night per pet, $5 per day fishing fee. Weekly and group rates available. Some credit cards accepted. Open year-round.

Directions: Drive on I-15 to Victorville and the exit for Bear Valley Road. Take that exit and drive east on Bear Valley Road for six miles to Ridgecrest. Turn left on Ridgecrest, drive three miles, and make a left into the park.

Contact: Mojave Narrows Regional Park, 760/245-2226, fax 760/245-7887, www.co.sanbernardino.ca.us/parks/mojave.htm.

38 HAVASU LANDING RESORT AND CASINO

Scenic rating: 6

on western shore of Lake Havasu

BEST (

Situated on the western shore of Lake Havasu, this full-service resort is run by the Chemehuevi Indian Tribe. It even includes a casino with slot machines and a card room. The resort is situated in a desert landscape in the Chemehuevi Valley. A boat shuttle operates from the resort to the London Bridge and Havasu City, Arizona. A mobile-home park is within the resort and an airstrip is nearby. Some of the RV sites are rented for the entire winter. Permits are required for off-road vehicles and can be obtained at the resort. This is one of the most popular boating areas in the southwestern United States. The lake is 45 miles long, covers 19,300 acres, and is at the low elevation of 482 feet. Havasu was created when the Parker Dam was built across the Colorado River.

Campsites, facilities: There are 180 sites with full hookups (30 and 50 amps) for RVs up to 35 feet, three large tent camping areas, and mobile home and RV rentals. Picnic tables, restrooms with flush toilets and showers, a dump station, coin laundry, picnic areas, restaurant and lounge, casino, 24-hour security, 24-hour marina with gas dock, bait and tackle, general store and deli, boat launches, boat slips, fish-cleaning room, dry storage, boat shuttle, and boat launch and retrieval service are available. An airport is nearby. Leashed pets are permitted.

Reservations, fees: Reservations are accepted at 800/307-3610. Sites are $25–30 per night for RV sites, $15–20 per night for tent sites, $2 per person per night for more than two people, and $6 per night for each additional vehicle. Holiday rates are higher. Weekly and monthly rates are available. A boat-launch fee is charged. Some credit cards accepted. Two ATMs are on-site. Open year-round.

Directions: From Needles, drive south on Highway 95 for 19 miles to Havasu Lake Road. Turn left and drive 17.5 miles to the resort on the right.

From Blythe, drive north on Highway 95 for 79 miles to Havasu Lake Road. Turn right and drive 17.5 miles to the resort on the right.

Contact: Havasu Landing Resort and Casino, 760/858-4593 or 800/307-3610, www. havasulanding.com. For general information about Lake Havasu, contact the Lake Havasu Tourism Bureau, 928/453-3444 or 800/2-HA-VASU (800/242-8278), www.golakehavasu. com; Lake Havasu Area Chamber of Commerce, 928/855-4115, www.havasuchamber. com.

39 BLACK MEADOW LANDING
🏊 🎣 🛥 🐎 🚐 ⛺

Scenic rating: 6

south of Lake Havasu on the Colorado River

This area of the Colorado River attracts a lot of people, so reservations are highly recommended. Hot weather, warm water, and proximity to Las Vegas make this one of the top camping and boating hot spots in the West. Vacationers are here year-round, although fewer people use it in the late winter. Black Meadow Landing is a large resort with hundreds of RV sites, lodging, and a long list of amenities. Once you arrive, everything you need for a stay should be available within the resort.

Campsites, facilities: There are 350 sites with full hookups (30 amps) for RVs up to 40 feet and tent camping is available. Park-model cabins, kitchen cabins, and a motel are also available. Restrooms with flush toilets and showers, drinking water, picnic tables, picnic areas, horseshoe pit, restaurant, convenience store, recreation room (winter only), bait and tackle, propane, full-service marina, boat launch, boat slips, boat and RV storage,

a swimming lagoon, and a five-hole golf course are available. Leashed pets are permitted.

Reservations, fees: Reservations are accepted at 800/7-HAVASU (800/742-8278). Sites are $25–60 per night, $6 per person per night for more than two people, $25 per night for tent sites, and $6 per night for each additional vehicle. Monthly rates are available. Some credit cards accepted. Open year-round.

Directions: From Southern California, take I-10 east to Blythe and turn north on U.S. 95. Continue to Vidal Junction at the intersection of U.S. 95 and Highway 62. Turn east on Highway 62 and drive to Earp and Parker Dam Road. Continue straight on Parker Dam Road and drive to a Y intersection and Black Meadow Landing Road (near Parker Dam). Bear left on Black Meadow Landing Road and drive approximately nine miles to the resort at the end of the road.

From Northern California, drive to Barstow and I-40. Turn east on I-40 and drive to Needles. Continue east on I-40 to Arizona Highway 95. Drive south on Arizona Highway 95 to Lake Havasu City. Continue south to the Parker Dam turnoff. Turn west and drive across the dam to a Y intersection and Black Meadow Landing Road. Bear right on Black Meadow Landing Road and drive approximately nine miles to the resort at the end of the road. Note: Towed vehicles are not allowed to cross the dam.

Contact: Black Meadow Landing, 760/663-4901, www.blackmeadowlanding.com. For general information about the Colorado River and Lake Havasu, contact the Lake Havasu Tourism Bureau, 928/453-3444 or 800/2-HA-VASU (800/242-8278), www.golakehavasu. com; Lake Havasu Area Chamber of Commerce, 928/855-4115, www.havasuchamber. com.

40 RIVERLAND RV PARK

Contact: Riverland RV Park, 760/663-3733, www.reynoldsresorts.com.

Scenic rating: 6

on the Colorado River near Parker Dam

This resort is in the middle of a very popular boating area, particularly for waterskiing. Summer is the busiest time because of the sunshine and warm water. In the winter, although temperatures can get pretty cold, around 40°F at night, the campground fills with retirees from the snow and rain country. Even though the resort is way out there on the Colorado River, there are plenty of services, including a convenience store, swimming beach, and full-service marina. Insider's tip: One of the best spots for catfish is a few miles down the road below Parker Dam.

Campsites, facilities: There are 60 sites with full hookups (50 amps) for RVs up to 40 feet. Picnic tables are provided. A park-model cabin is available. Restrooms with flush toilets and showers, drinking water, cable television, Wi-Fi, convenience store, coin laundry, full-service marina, boat launch, boat slips, boat and RV storage, swimming beach, fishing pier, bait, recreation room (winter only), and horseshoe pits are available. An ATM is within five miles and an 18-hole golf course is about 20 minutes away in Arizona. Leashed pets are permitted with restrictions.

Reservations, fees: Reservations are accepted at 760/663-3733. Sites are $35 per night on Friday and Saturday, $30 per night Sunday through Thursday, $40 on holidays. Monthly rates are available November through May. Some credit cards accepted. Open year-round.

Directions: From Southern California, take I-10 east to Blythe and turn north on U.S. 95. Continue to Vidal Junction at the intersection of U.S. 95 and Highway 62. Turn east on Highway 62 and drive to Earp and Parker Dam Road. Continue straight on Parker Dam Road and drive five miles to the resort on the right.

41 LOST LAKE RESORT

Scenic rating: 6

on the Colorado River in Parker Valley

If you're looking for a remote spot on the Colorado River, this is it. This is kind of like an oasis in the middle of the desert. Direct access to the Colorado River is provided, and this is one of the few places around that sell fishing licenses for this stretch of the Colorado River. The Parker Valley section of the river is part of the Colorado River Indian Reservation, and the tribe requires that all anglers obtain a permit. One of the best spots for big catfish, including large flathead catfish and channel catfish, is below Parker Dam. If you catch a razorback sucker, a rare event, it must be released. It is an endangered species. Note that about half of the sites are filled with long-term or permanent renters.

Campsites, facilities: There are 150 sites with full hookups (30 amps), including four premium sites. Tent camping is available. Picnic tables are provided at most sites. Restrooms with flush toilets, showers, coin laundry, convenience store, café, recreation room (winter only), boat and RV storage, boat launch, bait and tackle, fishing licenses, and full-service marina are available. Leashed pets are permitted.

Reservations, fees: Reservations are accepted at 760/664-4413. Sites are $30 per night per vehicle; the premium sites are $40 per night. Monthly rates are available in winter. Some credit cards accepted. Open year-round.

Directions: From Southern California, take I-10 east to Blythe and turn north on U.S. 95. Drive for 31 miles to the resort on the right.

Contact: Lost Lake Resort, 760/664-4413.

42 BLACK ROCK CANYON AND HORSE CAMP

🚶 🐴 ♿ 🚐 ⛺

Scenic rating: 4

in Joshua Tree National Park

This is the fanciest darn public campground this side of the desert. Why, it actually has drinking water. The camp is set at the mouth of Black Rock Canyon, at 4,000 feet elevation, which provides good winter hiking possibilities amid unique (in other words, weird) rock formations, about a half-hour drive from the campground. Show up in summer and you'll trade your gold for a sip of water. The camp is set near the excellent Black Rock Canyon Visitor Center and a trailhead for a four-mile round-trip hike to a rock wash. If you scramble onward, the route continues all the way to the top of Eureka Peak, at 5,518 feet, an 11-mile round-trip. But hey, why not just drive there?

Campsites, facilities: There are 100 sites for tents or RVs up to 35 feet (no hookups), and 15 equestrian sites for up to six people and four horses per site. Picnic tables and fire grills are provided. Drinking water, flush toilets, and dump station are available. The horse camp has hitching posts and a water faucet and no tents are allowed. Some facilities are wheelchair-accessible. Leashed pets are permitted, but not on trails.

Reservations, fees: Reservations are accepted at 877/444-6777 or www.recreation.gov ($10 reservation fee). Sites are $15 per night, plus $15 park entrance fee per vehicle. Open year-round, weather permitting.

Directions: From the junction of I-10 and Highway 62 near Palm Springs, drive northeast on Highway 62 for 22.5 miles to Yucca Valley and Joshua Lane. Turn right (south) on Joshua Lane and drive about five miles to the campground.

Contact: Joshua Tree National Park, 760/367-5500 or 760/362-4367; Black Rock Nature Center, 760/367-3001, www.nps.gov/jotr.

43 INDIAN COVE CAMPGROUND

🚶 🐴 🚐 ⛺

Scenic rating: 4

in Joshua Tree National Park

This is one of the campgrounds near the northern border of Joshua Tree National Park. The vast desert park, covering 1,238 square miles, is best known for its unique granite formations and scraggly-looking trees. If you had to withstand the summer heat here, you'd look scraggly too. Drinking water is available at the Indian Cove Ranger Station.

Campsites, facilities: There are 101 sites for tents or RVs up to 35 feet (no hookups), and a group camp with 13 sites for tents only for up to 60 people. Drinking water is available at the Indian Cove Ranger Station. Vault toilets, picnic tables, and fire grills are provided. Gas, groceries, and laundry services are available in Twentynine Palms (seven miles) or Joshua Tree (12 miles). Leashed pets are permitted, but not on trails.

Reservations, fees: Reservations are accepted at 800/365-CAMP (800/365-2267) or at http://reservations.nps.gov. Sites are $15 per night, $25–40 per night for group sites, plus $15 per vehicle park entrance fee. Open year-round.

Directions: From the junction of I-10 and Highway 62 near Palm Springs, drive northeast on Highway 62 for 22 miles to Yucca Valley, continue to the small town of Joshua Tree, and then continue nine miles to Indian Cove Road. Turn right and drive three miles to the campground.

Contact: Joshua Tree National Park, 760/367-5500 or 760/362-4367, fax 760/367-5546, www.nps.gov/jotr.

44 HIDDEN VALLEY

Scenic rating: 7

in Joshua Tree National Park

This is one of California's top campgrounds for rock-climbers. Set at 4,200 feet elevation in the high desert country, this is one of several camping options in the area. A trailhead is available two miles from camp at Barker Dam, an easy one-mile loop that features the Wonderland of Rocks. The hike takes you next to a small lake with magical reflections of rock formations off its surface. The RV sites here are snatched up quickly and this campground fills almost daily with rock-climbers.

Campsites, facilities: There are 45 sites for tents or RVs up to 25 feet (no hookups). Picnic tables and fire grills are provided. Vault toilets are available. No drinking water is available. Leashed pets are permitted.

Reservations, fees: No reservations are accepted. Sites are $10 per night, and $15 park entrance fee per vehicle. Open year-round.

Directions: From the junction of I-10 and Highway 62 near Palm Springs, drive northeast on Highway 62 for 22 miles to Yucca Valley, then continue to the small town of Joshua Tree and Park Boulevard. Turn south on Park Boulevard and drive 14 miles to the campground on the left.

Contact: Joshua Tree National Park, 760/367-5500 or 760/362-4367, fax 760/367-5546, www.nps.gov/jotr.

45 RYAN

Scenic rating: 4

in Joshua Tree National Park

This is one of the high desert camps in the immediate area (see also the *Jumbo Rocks* listing in this chapter). Joshua Tree National Park is a forbidding paradise: huge, hot, and waterless

(most of the time). The unique rock formations look as if some great artist made them with a chisel. The elevation is 4,300 feet. The best hike in the park starts here—a three-mile round-trip to Ryan Mountain is a 1,000-foot climb to the top at 5,470 feet elevation. The view is simply drop-dead gorgeous, not only of San Jacinto, Tahquitz, and San Gorgonio peaks, but of several beautiful rock-studded valleys as well as the Wonderland of Rocks.

Campsites, facilities: There are 31 sites for tents or RVs up to 25 feet (no hookups). Picnic tables and fire grills are provided. Vault toilets are available. No drinking water is available. Hitching posts are available (bring water for the horses). Leashed pets are permitted.

Reservations, fees: Reservations are accepted for equestrian sites only at 760/367-5541. Sites are $10 per night, and there is a $15 park entrance fee per vehicle. Open year-round.

Directions: From the junction of I-10 and Highway 62 near Palm Springs, drive northeast on Highway 62 to Twentynine Palms and Utah Trail. Turn right (south) on Utah Trail and drive about 20 miles to the campground entrance on the left.

Contact: Joshua Tree National Park, 760/367-5500 or 760/362-4367, fax 760/367-5546, www.nps.gov/jotr.

46 SHEEP PASS GROUP CAMP

Scenic rating: 4

in Joshua Tree National Park

Several campgrounds are in this stretch of high desert. Ryan campground (see listing in this chapter), just a couple of miles down the road, has an excellent trailhead for a trek to Ryan Mountain, the best hike in the park. Temperatures are routinely over 100°F here in the summer. (For details on this area, see the *White Tank* listing in this chapter.)

Campsites, facilities: There are six group

camps for tents or RVs up to 25 feet (no hookups) that can accommodate 20–50 people each. Picnic tables and fire grills are provided. Vault toilets are available. No drinking water is available. Leashed pets are permitted.

Reservations, fees: Reservations are accepted at 877/444-6777 or at www.recreation.gov ($10 reservation fee). Sites are $25–40 per night, plus $15 park entrance fee per vehicle. Open year-round.

Directions: From the junction of I-10 and Highway 62 near Palm Springs, drive northeast on Highway 62 to Twentynine Palms and Utah Trail. Turn right (south) on Utah Trail and drive about 16 miles to the campground on the left.

Contact: Joshua Tree National Park, 760/367-5500 or 760/362-4367, fax 760/367-5546, www.nps.gov/jotr.

47 JUMBO ROCKS

Scenic rating: 4

in Joshua Tree National Park

Joshua Tree National Park covers more than 1,238 square miles. It is striking high-desert country with unique granite formations that seem to change color at different times of the day. At 4,400 feet, this camp is one of the higher ones in the park, with adjacent boulders and rock formations that look as if they have been strewn about by an angry giant. It is a popular site for rock-climbing.

Campsites, facilities: There are 125 sites for tents or RVs up to 35 feet (no hookups). Picnic tables and fire grills are provided. Vault toilets are available. No drinking water is available. Leashed pets are permitted.

Reservations, fees: Reservations are not accepted. Sites are $10, and there is a $15 park entrance fee per vehicle. Open year-round.

Directions: From the junction of I-10 and Highway 62 near Palm Springs, drive northeast on Highway 62 to Twentynine Palms and

Utah Trail. Turn right (south) on Utah Trail and drive about nine miles to the campground on the left side of the road.

Contact: Joshua Tree National Park, 760/367-5500 or 760/362-4367, fax 760/367-5546, www.nps.gov/jotr.

48 BELLE

Scenic rating: 4

in Joshua Tree National Park

This camp is at 3,800 feet elevation in rocky high country. It is one of six camps in the immediate area. (For more details, see the *White Tank* listing in this chapter.)

Campsites, facilities: There are 18 sites for tents or RVs up to 35 feet (no hookups). Picnic tables and fire grills are provided. Vault toilets are available. No drinking water is available. Leashed pets are permitted.

Reservations, fees: No reservations are accepted. Sites are $10 per night, and there is a $15 park entrance fee per vehicle. Open year-round.

Directions: From the junction of I-10 and Highway 62 near Palm Springs, drive northeast on Highway 62 to Twentynine Palms and Utah Trail. Turn right (south) on Utah Trail and drive eight miles to Pinto Basin Road. Turn left (heading toward I-10) and drive about 1.5 miles to the campground on the left.

Contact: Joshua Tree National Park, 760/367-5500 or 760/362-4367, fax 760/367-5546, www.nps.gov/jotr.

49 WHITE TANK
🚶 🏕 🚐 ⛺

Scenic rating: 4

in Joshua Tree National Park

Joshua Tree National Park is a unique area where the high and low desert meet. Winter is a good time to explore the beautiful boulder piles and rock formations amid scraggly Joshua trees. There are several trails in the area, with the best near Black Rock Campground, Hidden Valley, and Cottonwood. The elevation is 3,800 feet.

Campsites, facilities: There are 15 sites for tents or RVs up to 25 feet (no hookups). Picnic tables and fire grills are provided. Vault toilets are available. No drinking water is available. Leashed pets are permitted.

Reservations, fees: No reservations are accepted. Sites are $10 per night, and there is $15 park entrance fee per vehicle. Open year-round.

Directions: From the junction of I-10 and Highway 62 near Palm Springs, drive northeast on Highway 62 to Twentynine Palms and Utah Trail. Turn right (south) on Utah Trail and drive eight miles to Pinto Basin Road. Turn left (heading toward I-10) and drive three miles to the campground on the left.

Contact: Joshua Tree National Park, 760/367-5500 or 760/362-4367, fax 760/367-5546, www.nps.gov/jotr.

50 COTTONWOOD
🚶 🏕 ♿ 🚐 ⛺

Scenic rating: 4

in Joshua Tree National Park

If you enter Joshua Tree National Park at its southern access point, this is the first camp you will reach. The park visitors center, where maps are available, is a mandatory stop. This park is vast, high-desert country, highlighted by unique rock formations, occasional scraggly trees, and vegetation that manages to survive the bleak, roasting summers. This camp is set at 3,000 feet elevation. A trailhead is available here for an easy one-mile nature trail, where small signs have been posted to identify different types of vegetation. You'll notice, however, that they all look like cacti (the plants, not the signs, heh, heh).

Campsites, facilities: There are 62 sites for tents or RVs up to 35 feet (no hookups), and a group campground with three sites for 15–20 people each. Picnic tables and fire grills are provided. Drinking water and flush toilets are available. Some facilities are wheelchair-accessible. Leashed pets are permitted.

Reservations, fees: Reservations are accepted for group sites only at 877/444-6777 or www.recreation.gov ($10 reservation fee). Sites are $15 per night, and group sites are $30 per night. Park entrance fee is $15 per vehicle. Open year-round.

Directions: From Indio, drive east on I-10 for 35 miles to the exit for Pinto Basin Road/Twentynine Palms (near Chiriaco Summit). Take that exit and drive north for seven miles (entering the park) to the campground on the right.

Contact: Joshua Tree National Park, 760/367-5500 or 760/362-4367, fax 760/367-5546, www.nps.gov/jotr.

51 SAM'S FAMILY SPA
🏊 〰 🏕 🏇 ♿ 🚐 ⛺

Scenic rating: 3

near Palm Springs

Hot mineral pools attract swarms of winter vacationers to the Palm Springs area. The therapeutic pools are partially enclosed. This 50-acre park, set 13 miles outside of Palm Springs, provides an alternative to the more crowded spots. And this is one of the few parks in the area that allows tent campers. A mobile-home park is adjacent to the RV park. The elevation of Sam's Family Spa is 1,000

CAMPING

feet. (For information on the tramway ride to Desert View west of Palm Springs, or the hike to Mount San Jacinto, see the *Sky Valley Resort* listing in this chapter.)

Campsites, facilities: There are 170 sites for tents and RVs up to 42 feet (with full hook-ups of 30 and 50 amps). Four mobile-home rentals and a motel are also available. Picnic tables are provided. There is a separate area with barbecues. Restrooms with showers, playground, heated swimming pool, heated wading pool, four hot mineral pools, sauna, Wi-Fi, coin laundry, and convenience store are available. Some facilities are wheelchair-accessible. Leashed pets are permitted in the campground only.

Reservations, fees: Reservations are accepted online only; no telephone reservations. Sites are $40 per night. Weekly and monthly rates available. Some credit cards accepted. Open year-round.

Directions: Drive on I-10 to the Palm Springs Area and the Palm Drive exit (to Desert Hot Springs). Take that exit and drive north on Palm Drive for about two miles to Dillon Road. Turn right (east) on Dillon Road and drive 4.5 miles to the park on the right (70–875 Dillon Road).

Contact: Sam's Family Spa, 760/329-6457, fax 760/329-8267, www.samsfamilyspa.com.

52 SKY VALLEY RESORT

🏃 🏊 ♨ 🐕 🚵 ♿ 🚐

Scenic rating: 2

near Palm Springs

This 140-acre park is much like a small town, complete with RV homes, an RV park, and park-model rentals and seasonal restaurants. One of the best adventures in California is just west of Palm Springs, taking the aerial tram up from Chino Canyon to Desert View, a ride/climb of 2,600 feet for remarkable views to the east across the desert below. An option from there is hiking the flank of Mount

San Jacinto, including making the ascent to the summit (10,804 feet), a round-trip butt-kicker of nearly 12 miles. Golf courses are nearby. Note that there are 260 permanent residents.

Campsites, facilities: There are 618 sites with full hookups (30 and 50 amps) for RVs up to 42 feet. No tents allowed. Restrooms with showers, cable TV, four swimming pools, nine natural hot mineral whirlpools, two laundry rooms, two large recreation rooms, fitness centers, children's playroom, seasonal grocery store, chapel program, seasonal tennis and golf lessons, pickleball court, business center with modem access, Wi-Fi, social director, shuffleboard, tennis, horseshoes, crafts room, and walking paths are available. Propane gas is nearby. Some facilities are wheelchair-accessible. Leashed pets are permitted.

Reservations, fees: Reservations are accepted at 888/893-7727 or by website. Sites are $48–49 per night, $38–39.50 in off-season, $5 per person per night for more than two people. Monthly rates available. Some credit cards accepted. Open year-round.

Directions: Drive on I-10 to the Palm Springs area and the Palm Drive exit (to Desert Hot Springs). Take that exit and drive north on Palm Drive for three miles to Dillon Road. Turn right on Dillon Road and drive 8.5 miles to the park on the right (74–711 Dillon Road).

Contact: Sky Valley Resort, 760/329-2909, fax 760/329-9473, www.skyvalleyresort.com.

53 HAPPY TRAVELER RV PARK

🏊 🐕 🚐

Scenic rating: 1

in Palm Springs

Are we having fun yet? They are at Happy Traveler, which is within walking distance of Palm Springs shopping areas and restaurants. The Palm Springs Air Museum has a collection of World War II aircraft. A casino is one mile away.

Campsites, facilities: There are 130 sites with full hookups (30 and 50 amps) for RVs up to 40 feet. No tents or tent trailers. Picnic tables are provided. Restrooms with showers, cable TV, Wi-Fi, swimming pool, spa, clubhouse, shuffleboard, propane, seasonal activities, and coin laundry are available. Leashed pets are permitted with restrictions, including a maximum of two pets.

Reservations, fees: Reservations are accepted. Sites are $38 per night. Monthly rates available. Credit cards are not accepted. Open year-round.

Directions: Drive on I-10 to Palm Springs and Highway 111/Palm Canyon Drive. Take Palm Canyon Drive and drive 12 miles south to Mesquite Avenue. Turn right on Mesquite Avenue and drive to the park on the left (211 West Mesquite).

Contact: Happy Traveler RV Park, 760/325-8518, www.happytravelerrv.com.

54 OUTDOOR RESORT OF PALM SPRINGS
🏊 🐾 ♿ 🚐

Scenic rating: 6

near Palm Springs

This is considered a five-star resort, beautifully landscaped, huge, and offering many activities: swimming pools galore, 27-hole golf course, tons of tennis courts, spas, and on and on. The 137-acre park is four miles from Palm Springs. Note that this is a lot-ownership park with lots for sale. About a quarter of the sites are available for rent to vacationers. One of the best adventures in California is just west of Palm Springs: taking the aerial tram up from Chino Canyon to Desert View, a ride/climb of 2,600 feet for remarkable views to the east across the desert below.

Campsites, facilities: There are 1,213 sites with full hookups (30 and 50 amps) for RVs

up to 45 feet. No tent camping. RV rentals are also available. Restrooms with showers, eight swimming pools, spas, 14 lighted tennis courts, 27-hole golf course, two clubhouses, snack bar, café, beauty salon, coin laundry, Wi-Fi, modem access, convenience store, shuffleboard, and planned activities are available. Some facilities are wheelchair-accessible. Leashed pets are permitted.

Reservations, fees: Reservations are accepted at 800/843-3131 (California only). Sites are $67–77 per night, $1 per pet per night with a two-pet maximum. RV rentals are $95–115 per night. Monthly rates available. Some credit cards accepted. Open year-round.

Directions: Drive on I-10 to the Palm Springs area and continue to Cathedral City and the exit for Date Palm Drive. Take that exit and drive south on Date Palm Drive for two miles to Ramon Road. Turn left and drive to the resort on the right (69–411 Ramon Road).

Contact: Outdoor Resort, 760/324-4005, www.outdoorresort.com.

55 PALM SPRINGS OASIS RV PARK
🏊 🐾 ♿ 🚐

Scenic rating: 2

in Cathedral City

This popular wintering spot is for RV cruisers looking to hole up in the Palm Springs area for awhile. Palm Springs is only six miles away. This is a seniors-only park, meaning that you need to be at the magic age of 55 or above to qualify for a stay.

Campsites, facilities: There are 140 sites with full hookups (30 and 50 amps) for RVs up to 45 feet. No tents. Restrooms with showers, cable TV, Wi-Fi, modem access, two swimming pools, spa, tennis courts, coin laundry, and propane gas are available. An 18-hole golf course is adjacent to the park. Some facilities are wheelchair-accessible. Children and people under age 55 are not allowed. Leashed pets are permitted, with a two-pet maximum.

Reservations, fees: Reservations are accepted. Sites are $41 per night, $2 per person per night for more than two people. Weekly and monthly rates available. Some credit cards accepted. Open year-round.

Directions: Drive on I-10 to the Palm Springs area and continue to Cathedral City and the exit for Date Palm Drive. Take that exit and drive south on Date Palm Drive for four miles to Gerald Ford Drive and the park on the left corner (36–100 Date Palm Drive).

Contact: Palm Springs Oasis RV Park, 760/328-4813 or 800/680-0144, fax 760/328-8455.

56 INDIAN WELLS RV RESORT

Scenic rating: 2

in Indio

Indio is a good-sized town midway between the Salton Sea to the south and Palm Springs to the north, which is about 20 miles away. In the summer, it is one of the hottest places in America. In the winter, it is a favorite for "snowbirds," that is, RV and trailer owners from the snow country who migrate south for the winter. About half of the sites are filled with long-term renters.

Campsites, facilities: There are 381 sites with full hookups (50 amps) for RVs up to 45 feet; most are pull-through. No tents. Restrooms with showers, cable TV, Wi-Fi, three swimming pools, two therapy pools, horseshoes, basketball, volleyball, shuffleboard courts, putting green, planned activities, ice, dog run, picnic area, and coin laundry are available. Some facilities are wheelchair-accessible. Leashed pets are permitted, with a maximum of two.

Reservations, fees: Reservations are accepted at 800/789-0895. Sites are $46 per

night, $2.50 per person per night for more than two people. Weekly and monthly rates available. Some credit cards accepted. Open year-round.

Directions: Drive on I-10 to Indio and the exit for Jefferson Street. Take that exit, stay in the right lane, and drive to the light at Jefferson. Turn right at Jefferson and drive south for three miles to the park on the left (47–340 Jefferson Street).

Contact: Indian Wells RV Resort, 760/347-0895, fax 760/775-1147, www.carefreervresorts.com.

57 OUTDOOR RESORTS INDIO

Scenic rating: 7

in Indio

For owners of tour buses, motor coaches, and lavish RVs, it doesn't get any better than this in Southern California. Only RVers in Class A motor homes are allowed here. This resort bills itself as the "ultimate RV resort" and has been featured on the Travel Channel and in the Wall Street Journal. About 25 percent of the sites are available for rent; the other sites are owned by RVers. This park is set close to golf, shopping, and restaurants. Jeep tours of the surrounding desert canyons and organized recreation events are offered.

Campsites, facilities: There are 419 sites with full hookups (50 amps) for Class A motor homes with a minimum length of 28 feet. No trailers or pickup-truck campers. Restrooms with showers, cable TV, Wi-Fi, modem access, swimming pools, tennis courts, sauna, spas, massage service, hair salon, café, fitness center, clubhouse, coin laundry, and 18-hole golf course are available. Some facilities are wheelchair-accessible. Leashed pets are permitted, with a two-pet maximum.

Reservations, fees: Reservations are accepted. The winter rates are $65–75 per night, plus

$5 for electricity; summer rates are $40–50 per night, plus $7 for electricity. Some credit cards accepted. Open year-round.

Directions: Drive on I-10 to Indio and the exit for Indio Boulevard/Jefferson Street. Take that exit, stay in the right lane, and drive to the light at Jefferson. Turn right at Jefferson and drive south for three miles to Avenue 48. Turn left and drive 0.25 mile to the park on the left side of the road (80–394 Avenue 48).

Contact: Outdoor Resorts Indio, 760/775-7255 or 800/892-2992 (outside California), www.outdoorresortsindio.com.

58 MIDLAND LONG TERM VISITOR AREA

Scenic rating: 4

west of Blythe

Like its neighbor to the south (Mule Mountain), this camp is attractive to snowbirds, rockhounds (geodes and agates can be collected), and stargazers. The campground is on the southwest slope of the Big Maria Mountains, a designated wilderness, set at an elevation of 250 feet. The campsites are situated on flattened desert pavements consisting of alluvium. The desert landscape is extremely stark.

Campsites, facilities: There are numerous dispersed sites for tents or RVs of any length (no hookups). No drinking water or toilets are available. A dump station is nearby and is available mid-September through mid-April. Leashed pets are permitted.

Reservations, fees: Reservations are not accepted. The fee is $40 for up to 14 nights, $180 per season. Fees charged September 15 through April 15. Summer is free, with a 14-day limit. Open year-round.

Directions: From Blythe, drive east on I-10 a short distance to Lovekin Boulevard. Turn left and drive about eight miles to the campground on the right.

Contact: Bureau of Land Management, Palm Springs Field Office, 760/251-4800, fax 760/251-4899, www.blm.gov/ca.

59 MAYFLOWER COUNTY PARK

Scenic rating: 6

on the Colorado River

The Colorado River is the fountain of life around these parts and, for campers, the main attraction of this county park. It is a popular spot for waterskiing. There is river access here in the Blythe area. Fishing is good for channel and flathead catfish, striped bass, large- and smallmouth bass, bluegill, and crappie. This span of water is flanked by agricultural lands, although there are several developed recreation areas on the California side of the river south of Blythe near Palo Verde.

Campsites, facilities: There are 25 tent sites and 152 sites for RVs of any length (with partial hookups of 30 and 50 amps). Picnic tables and fire grills are provided. Drinking water, restrooms with flush toilets and free showers, dump station, and boat ramp are available. Some facilities are wheelchair-accessible. Leashed pets are permitted.

Reservations, fees: Reservations are not accepted. Sites are $16–18 per night, $2 boat launch fee, $1 per pet per night. Monthly rates available. Some credit cards accepted. Open year-round.

Directions: Drive on I-10 to Blythe and Highway 95. Take Highway 95 north (it becomes Intake Boulevard) and drive 3.5 miles to 6th Avenue. Turn right at 6th Avenue and drive 2.5 miles to Colorado River Road. Bear left and drive 0.5 mile to the park entrance.

Contact: Mayflower County Park, 760/922-4665, fax 760/922-9177, www.riversidecountyparks.org.

CAMPING

60 BLYTHE/COLORADO RIVER KOA

Scenic rating: 6

near the Colorado River

This RV park is set up for camper-boaters who want to hunker down for awhile along the Colorado River and cool off. Access to the park is easy off I-10, and a marina is available, both big pluses for those showing up with trailered boats. Swimming lagoons are another bonus. A golf course is within 10 miles. Note that about half of the sites are rented year-round.

Campsites, facilities: There are 287 sites for RVs of any length (with full hookups of 30 and 50 amps); some sites are pull-through. Tents are allowed, and seven park-model cabins are available. Picnic tables are provided. Restrooms with showers, heated swimming pool, spa, cable TV, Wi-Fi, modem access, coin laundry, telephone room, convenience store, card room, 24-hour security, RV and boat storage, arcade, recreation center, boat ramps, boat fuel, and propane gas are available. Some facilities are wheelchair-accessible. Leashed pets are permitted, with certain restrictions.

Reservations, fees: Reservations are accepted at 800/562-3948. Sites are $55.37 per night on Friday and Saturday, $45.37 per night Sunday through Thursday, $2 per person for more than four adults, $10 per night for each additional vehicle. Tent sites are $20 per night. Holiday rates are higher. Monthly rates available. Credit cards accepted. Open year-round.

Directions: Drive on I-10 to Blythe and continue east for two miles to the exit for Riviera Drive. Take that exit east and drive two miles to the park on the right (14100 Riviera Drive).

Contact: Blythe/Colorado River KOA, 14100 Riviera Dr., 760/922-5350, fax 760/922-1134, www.koa.com.

61 DESTINY McINTYRE RV RESORT

Scenic rating: 3

on the Colorado River

This RV park sits on the outskirts of Blythe on the Colorado River, with this stretch of river providing good conditions for boating, waterskiing, and other water sports. A swimming lagoon is a big plus, along with riverfront beach access. Fishing is an option, with a variety of fish, including striped bass, largemouth bass, and catfish, providing fair results.

Campsites, facilities: There are 40 tent sites and 160 sites with full hookups (30 and 50 amps) for RVs of any length, including 11 pull-through sites. Picnic tables and fire rings are provided. Drinking water, restrooms with flush toilets and showers, dump station, propane gas, store, bait, ice, and boat ramp and boat fuel are available. Some facilities are wheelchair-accessible. Leashed pets are permitted November through April only.

Reservations, fees: Reservations are accepted at 800/RV-DESTINY (800/783-3784). Sites are $20–37 per night or $10–19 during off-season (Nov.–Mar.), $4 per person per night for more than two people, $10 per night for each additional vehicle. Monthly rates available. Some credit cards accepted. Open year-round.

Directions: Drive on I-10 to Blythe to the exit for Intake Boulevard south. Take that exit and drive south on Intake Boulevard for 6.5 miles to the junction with 26th Avenue (it takes off to the right) and the park entrance on the left. Turn left and enter the park.

Contact: Destiny McIntyre RV Resort, 760/922-8205, fax 760/922-5695, www.destinyrv.com/mcintyrervresort.htm.

62 PALO VERDE COUNTY PARK

👣 🏊 🚣 🎣 🐕 🚐 ⛺

Scenic rating: 5

near the Colorado River

This is the only game in town, with no other camp around for many miles. It is set near a bend in the Colorado River, not far from the Cibola National Wildlife Refuge. A boat ramp is available at the park, making it a launch point for adventure. This stretch of river is a good one for powerboating and waterskiing. The best facilities for visitors are available here and on the west side of the river between Palo Verde and Blythe, with nothing available on the east side of the river.

Campsites, facilities: There are 20 sites for tents or RVs of any length (no hookups). Picnic tables, fire rings, restrooms with flush toilets, and shade ramadas are available. No drinking water. A boat ramp is available. A store, coin laundry, and propane gas are available in Palo Verde. Leashed pets are permitted.

Reservations, fees: Reservations are not accepted. There is no fee for camping. A three-day limit is enforced. Open year-round.

Directions: Drive on I-10 to Highway 78 (two miles west of Blythe). Take Highway 78 south and drive about 20 miles (three miles past Palo Verde) to the park entrance road on the east side.

Contact: Palo Verde County Park, Imperial County, 760/482-4462.

63 MULE MOUNTAIN LONG TERM VISITOR AREA

👣 🐕 🚐 ⛺

Scenic rating: 4

west of Blythe

Mule Mountain is out in the middle of nowhere, but rockhounds and stargazers have found it anyway; it's ideal for both activities.

There are two campgrounds, Coon Hollow and Wiley's Well, along with dispersed camping. Rockhounding, in particular, can be outstanding, with several geode and agate beds nearby. Hobby rock-collecting is permitted. Commercial rock-poaching is not. The site, ideal for winter camping, attracts snowbirds and is set in a desert landscape at an elevation of 150 feet. Bradshaw Trail runs east to west through the visitors area.

Campsites, facilities: There are 28 sites at Coon Hollow and 14 sites at Wiley's Well for tents or RVs up to 35 feet (no hookups). Picnic tables and fire grills are provided. Vault toilets are available. No drinking water is available. A dump station is nearby, halfway between the two campgrounds, and is available mid-September through mid-April. Leashed pets are permitted.

Reservations, fees: Reservations are not accepted. Sites are $40 for up to 14 nights, $180 per season, with a 14-day stay limit every 28 days. Open year-round.

Directions: From Blythe, drive west on I-10 about 15 miles to Wiley's Well Road. Turn left (south) and drive about nine miles (the road turns to dirt) to Wiley's Well. Continue another three miles to reach Coon Hollow. Dispersed camping is allowed once you pass the sign that indicates you're in the visitors center.

Contact: Bureau of Land Management, Palm Springs Field Office, 760/251-4800, fax 760/251-4899, www.blm.gov.

64 TOOL BOX SPRING

👣 🐕 ⛺

Scenic rating: 5

in San Bernardino National Forest

This is a lightly used campground well off the beaten track. More like off the beaten universe. That makes it perfect for people who want to be by themselves when they go camping. Ramona Trail begins at the campground, heads out to the north, and provides a 3.5-mile one-way hike, with a 1,500-foot loss and then gain in elevation. In the winter, call for road conditions to determine accessibility. The elevation is 6,500 feet.

Campsites, facilities: There are six tent sites as well as disbursed camping. Picnic tables and fire grills are provided. Vault toilets are available. Drinking water is available intermittently; check for current status. Garbage must be packed out. Leashed pets are permitted.

Reservations, fees: No reservations accepted and there is no camping fee. An Adventure Pass ($30 annual fee or $5 daily pass) per parked vehicle is required. Open year-round, but subject to closure during fire season.

Directions: From Hemet, drive east on Highway 74 into San Bernardino National Forest and continue just past Lake Hemet to Forest Road 6S13. Turn right on Forest Road 6S13 (paved, then dirt) and drive four miles to a fork. Bear left at the fork and continue on Forest Road 6S13 for 4.5 miles to the camp on the left.

Contact: San Bernardino National Forest, San Jacinto Ranger District, 909/382-2921, fax 951/659-2107.

65 PINYON FLAT

Scenic rating: 6

near Cahuilla Tewanet Vista Point in San Bernardino National Forest

The Cahuilla Tewanet Vista Point is just two miles east of the camp and provides a good, easy side trip, along with a sweeping view to the east of the desert on clear days. A primitive trail is available two miles away to the southeast via Forest Road 7S01 off a short spur road (look for it on the left side of the road). This hike crosses a mix of sparse forest and high-desert terrain for 10 miles, passing Cactus Spring five miles in. Desert bighorn

sheep are sometimes spotted in this area. The elevation is 4,000 feet.

Campsites, facilities: There are 18 sites for tents or RVs up to 15 feet (no hookups). Picnic tables and fire rings are provided. Drinking water and vault toilets are available. Some facilities are wheelchair-accessible. Leashed pets are permitted.

Reservations, fees: Reservations are not accepted. Sites are $8 per night. Open year-round.

Directions: Drive on I-10 to Palm Springs and Highway 111. Turn south on Highway 111 and drive to Rancho Mirage and Highway 74. Turn right (south) on Highway 74 and drive 14 miles (a slow, twisty road) to the campground on the right.

Contact: San Bernardino National Forest, San Jacinto Ranger District, 909/382-2921, fax 951/659-2107.

66 LAKE CAHUILLA COUNTY PARK

Scenic rating: 7

near Indio

Lake Cahuilla covers just 135 acres, but those are the most loved 135 acres for miles in all directions. After all, water out here is as scarce as polar bears. This 710-acre Riverside County park provides large palm trees and a 10-acre beach and water-play area. In the winter it is stocked with trout, and in the summer with catfish. Other species include largemouth and striped bass, crappie, and carp to 30 pounds. No swimming is allowed. Only car-top boats are permitted (no gas motors), and a speed limit of 10 mph is enforced. An equestrian camp is also available, complete with corrals. Equestrian and hiking trails are available on nearby public land. Morrow Trail is popular, and the trailhead is near the park's ranger station. A warning: The wind can really howl through here, and temperatures well over 100°F are typical in the summer.

Campsites, facilities: There are 55 sites with partial hookups (30 and 50 amps) and 10 sites with no hookups for RVs, a primitive camping area with no hookups for tents or RVs, and a large group area with horse corrals. Maximum RV length is 45 feet. Fire grills and picnic tables are provided. Restrooms with showers, dump station, seasonal swimming pool, and a primitive (hand-launch) beach boat launch are available. No gas motors are allowed. Some facilities are wheelchair-accessible. Leashed pets are permitted.

Reservations, fees: Reservations are accepted at 800/234-PARK (800/234-7275; $7.50 reservation fee). Sites are $13–18 per night, $1 per pet per night. Weekly rates are available during the winter. Maximum stay is two weeks. Some credit cards accepted. Open year-round, closed Tuesday, Wednesday, and Thursday May through October.

Directions: Drive on I-10 to Indio and the exit for Monroe Street. Take that exit and drive south on Monroe Street to Avenue 58. Turn right (west) and drive two miles to the park at the end of the road.

Contact: Lake Cahuilla County Park, 760/564-4712, fax 760/564-2506, www.riversidecountyparks.org.

67 HEADQUARTERS

🚶 🚲 🏊 🛶 🎣 🐎 ♿ �car ⛺

Scenic rating: 5

in the Salton Sea State Recreation Area

This is the northernmost camp on the shore of the giant Salton Sea, one of the campgrounds at the Salton Sea State Recreation Area. Salton Sea is a vast, shallow, and unique lake, the center of a 360-square-mile basin and one of the world's inland seas. Salton Sea was created in 1905 when a dike broke, and in turn, the basin was flooded with saltwater. The lake is 35 miles long, but it has an average depth

of just 15 feet. It is set at the recreation area headquarters, just south of the town of Desert Beach at an elevation of 227 feet below sea level. Fishing for tilapia is popular, and it is also one of Southern California's most popular boating areas. Because of the low altitude, atmospheric pressure allows high performance for many ski boats. If winds are hazardous, a red beacon on the northeast shore of the lake will flash. If you see it, get to the nearest shore. The Salton Sea is about a three-hour drive from Los Angeles. Use is moderate year-round, but lowest in the summer because of temperatures that can hover in the 110°F range for days.

Campsites, facilities: There are 25 sites with no hookups for tents or RVs, 15 with full hookups (30 amps) for RVs up to 40 feet, and several hike-in/bike-in sites. Picnic tables, fire grills, and shade ramadas are provided. Drinking water, restrooms with flush toilets and coin showers, dump station, fish cleaning station, and visitors center with Wi-Fi access are available. A store is within two miles. Some facilities are wheelchair-accessible. Leashed pets are permitted in the campgrounds and on roadways only.

Reservations, fees: Reservations are accepted at 800/444-PARK (800/444-7275) or www.reserveamerica.com ($7.50 reservation fee). Sites are $17–23 per night, and $2 per person per night for hike-in/bike-in sites. Boat launching is $3 per day. Open year-round.

Directions: From the Los Angeles area, take I-10 east to Indio and the exit for the Highway 86 Expressway. Take that exit and drive south for 12 miles to 66th Avenue. Turn left and drive less than one mile to Mecca and Highway 111. Turn right (south) on Highway 111 and drive 12 miles to the entrance on the right.

Contact: Salton Sea State Recreation Area, 760/393-3052 or 760/393-3059, www.parks.ca.gov.

68 MECCA BEACH

🥾 🚴 🏊 🛶 🚤 🐕 ♿ 🚐 ⛺

Scenic rating: 4

in the Salton Sea State Recreation Area

This is one of the camps set in the Salton Sea State Recreation Area on the northeastern shore of the lake. The big attractions here are the waterfront sites, which are not available at nearby Headquarters campground (see listing in this chapter).

Campsites, facilities: There are 110 sites, 10 with full hookups (30 amps) for tents or RVs of any length, and several hike-in/bike-in sites. Picnic tables and fire grills are provided. Drinking water, restrooms with flush toilets and showers, amphitheater, and a fish cleaning station are available. A dump station is one mile north of Headquarters campground and a store is within 3.5 miles. Some facilities are wheelchair-accessible. Leashed pets are permitted in the campgrounds and roadways only.

Reservations, fees: Reservations are accepted at 800/444-PARK (800/444-7275) or www.reserveamerica.com ($7.50 reservation fee). Sites are $17–23 per night, $2 per person per night for hike-in/bike-in sites. Boat launching is $3 per day. Open year-round.

Directions: From the Los Angeles area, take I-10 east to Indio and the exit for the Highway 86 Expressway. Take that exit and drive south for 12 miles to 66th Avenue. Turn left and drive less than one mile to Mecca and Highway 111. Turn right (south) on Highway 111 and drive 12.5 miles to the entrance on the right.

Contact: Salton Sea State Recreation Area, 760/393-3052 or 760/393-3059, www.parks.ca.gov.

69 CORVINA BEACH

🥾 🚴 🏊 🛶 🚤 🐕 ♿ 🚐 ⛺

Scenic rating: 5

in the Salton Sea State Recreation Area

This is by far the biggest of the campgrounds on the Salton Sea. The campground is actually more of an open area on hard-packed dirt, best for parking an RV. (For details about the Salton Sea, see the *Headquarters* listing in this chapter.)

Campsites, facilities: There are 250 primitive sites in an open area for tents or RVs of any length (no hookups) and some hike-in/bike-in sites. Drinking water and chemical toilets are available. Fires are permitted in metal containers only. A store and gas station are available within five miles. Leashed pets are permitted in the campground and on roadways only.

Reservations, fees: Reservations are not accepted. Sites are $7 per night, $2 per person per night for hike-in/bike-in sites. Boat launching is $3 per day. Open year-round.

Directions: From the Los Angeles area, take I-10 east to Indio and the exit for the Highway 86 Expressway. Take that exit and drive south for 12 miles to 66th Avenue. Turn left and drive less than one mile to Mecca and Highway 111. Turn right (south) on Highway 111 and drive 14 miles to the entrance on the right.

Contact: Salton Sea State Recreation Area, 760/393-3052 or 760/393-3059, www.parks.ca.gov.

70 SALT CREEK PRIMITIVE AREA

🥾 🚴 🏊 🛶 🚤 🐕 ♿ 🚐 ⛺

Scenic rating: 4

in the Salton Sea State Recreation Area

Waterfront campsites are a bonus at this campground, even though the campground consists of just an open area on hard-packed dirt. Birding hikes are available during winter months. Several trails leave from camp, or nearby the camp, and head 1–2 miles to the Bat Cave Buttes, which are in the Durmid Hills on Bureau of Land Management property. There are bats in the numerous caves to explore, although the nearby OHV traffic has reduced their numbers. From the buttes, which are up to 100 feet above sea level, hikers can see both the north and south ends of the Salton Sea simultaneously. This is the only easily accessible place to view both shores of the Salton Sea. Many people believe the buttes are the southernmost point of the San Andreas Fault; the fault does not exist above ground south of here. (For details on the Salton Sea State Recreation Area, see the *Headquarters* listing in this chapter.)

Campsites, facilities: There are 200 primitive sites for tents or RVs of any length (no hookups) and several hike-in/bike-in sites. Drinking water and chemical toilets are available. Fires are permitted in metal containers only. Leashed pets are permitted in the campgrounds and on roadways only.

Reservations, fees: Reservations are not accepted. Sites are $7 per night, $2 per person per night for hike-in/bike-in sites. Open year-round.

Directions: From the Los Angeles area, take I-10 east to Indio and the exit for the Highway 86 Expressway. Take that exit and drive south for 12 miles to 66th Avenue. Turn left and drive less than one mile to Mecca and Highway 111. Turn right (south) on Highway 111 and drive 17.5 miles to the entrance on the right.

Contact: Salton Sea State Recreation Area, 760/393-3052 or 760/393-3059, www.parks.ca.gov.

71 FOUNTAIN OF YOUTH SPA

🏊 🚴 ♨️ 🏕️ ♿ 🚐 ⛺

Scenic rating: 4

near the Salton Sea

Natural artesian steam rooms are the highlight here, but close inspection reveals that nobody seems to be getting any younger. This is a vast private park on 90 acres, set near the Salton Sea. Though this park has 1,000 sites for RVs, almost half of the sites have seasonal renters. This park is popular with snowbird campers and about 2,000 people live here during the winter. (See the *Red Hill Marina County Park* listing in this chapter for side-trip options.)

Campsites, facilities: There are 835 sites with full hookups (30 and 50 amps) and 165 sites with no hookups for tents or RVs. Restrooms with flush toilets and showers, cable TV, natural artesian steam rooms, swimming pools, artesian mineral water spa, three freshwater spas, recreation halls, dump stations, fitness room, library, picnic areas, nine-hole desert-style golf course, horseshoes, organized activities, craft and sewing room, Wi-Fi, modem access, coin laundry, beauty parlor, masseur, church services, propane gas, and groceries are available. Some facilities are wheelchair-accessible. Leashed pets are permitted.

Reservations, fees: No reservations accepted. Winter rates are $15–42 per night, summer rates are $15–35 per night, $1 per person per night for more than two people. Weekly and monthly rates available. Some credit cards accepted. Open year-round.

Directions: From the Los Angeles area, take I-10 east to Indio and the exit for the Highway 86 Expressway. Take that exit and drive south for 12 miles to Avenue 62. Turn right and drive less than one mile to Highway 111. Turn left (south) on Highway 111 and drive 44 miles to Hot Mineral Spa Road. Turn left (north) on Hot Mineral Spa Road and drive approximately four miles to Spa Road. Turn right and drive approximately 1.5 miles to the park on the left.

From Calipatria, drive north on Highway

111 to Niland, and then continue north for 15 miles to Hot Mineral Spa Road. Turn right (north) on Hot Mineral Spa Road and drive approximately four miles to Spa Road. Turn right and drive about 1.5 miles to the park on the left.

Contact: Fountain of Youth Spa, 888/8000-SPA (888/800-0772) or 760/354-1340, fax 760/354-1558, www.foyspa.com.

72 CORN SPRINGS

Scenic rating: 4

in BLM desert

Just think: If you spend a night here, you can say to darn near anybody, "I've camped someplace you haven't." I don't know whether to offer my condolences or congratulations, but Corn Springs offers a primitive spot in the middle of nowhere in desert country. A 0.5-mile interpretive trail can easily be walked in tennis shoes. It is divided into 11 stops with different vegetation, wildlife habitat, and cultural notes at each stop. The side trip to Joshua Tree National Park to the north (40-minute drive to closest entrance) is also well worth the adventure. So is the aerial tram ride available west of Palm Springs (one-hour drive) for an incredible view of the desert. On the other hand, if it's a summer afternoon, tell me, just how do you spend the day here when it's 115°F?

Campsites, facilities: There are nine sites for tents or RVs up to 22 feet (no hookups) and one group site for tents or RVs (one or two only) up to 22 feet that can accommodate up to 25 people. Picnic tables and fire grills are provided. Drinking water, shade ramadas, and vault toilets are available. Leashed pets are permitted.

Reservations, fees: Reservations are not accepted. Sites are $6 per night. Open year-round.

Directions: From Indio, drive east on I-10

for 60 miles to the Corn Springs Road exit. Take that exit to Old Chuckwalla Valley Road. Turn right (south) onto Old Chuckwalla Valley Road and drive 0.5 mile to Corn Springs Road. Turn right and drive 10 miles on a dirt road to the campground on the left.

Contact: Bureau of Land Management, Palm Springs Field Office, 760/251-4800, fax 760/251-4899, www.blm.gov/ca.

73 BOMBAY BEACH

Scenic rating: 5

in the Salton Sea State Recreation Area

All in all, this is a strange-looking place, with the Salton Sea, a vast body of water, surrounded by stark, barren countryside. This camp is set in a bay along the northeastern shoreline, where a beach and nature trails are available. The campground is a flat, open area. Nearby to the south is the Wister Waterfowl Management Area. The Salton Sea is California's unique saltwater lake set below sea level, with fishing for tilapia a possibility.

Campsites, facilities: There are 200 sites for tents or RVs of any length (no hookups) and several hike-in/bike-in sites. Drinking water and chemical toilets are available. Fires are permitted in metal containers only. A store, restaurant, marina, and boat launch are available nearby in Bombay Beach. Leashed pets are permitted.

Reservations, fees: Reservations are not accepted. Sites are $7 per night, $2 per person per night for hike-in/bike-in sites. Open year-round.

Directions: From the Los Angeles area, take I-10 east to Indio and the exit for the Highway 86 Expressway. Take that exit and drive south for 12 miles to 66th Avenue. Turn left and drive less than one mile to Mecca and Highway 111. Turn right (south) on Highway

111 and drive 25 miles to the campground entrance on the right.

From Calipatria, drive north on Highway 111 to Niland, then continue north 18 miles to the entrance on the left.

Contact: Salton Sea State Recreation Area, 760/393-3052 or 760/393-3059, www.parks. ca.gov.

74 RED HILL MARINA COUNTY PARK

Scenic rating: 3

near the Salton Sea

It's called Red Hill Marina, but you won't find a marina here; it washed away in the mid-1970s. This county park is near the south end of the Salton Sea, one of the weirdest places on earth. Set 228 feet below sea level, it's a vast body of water covering 360 square miles, 35 miles long, but with an average depth of just 15 feet. It's an extremely odd place to swim, as you bob around effortlessly in the highly saline water. Note that swimming is not recommended in this park because of the muddy shore. Fishing is often good for corvina in spring and early summer. Hundreds of species of birds stop by this area as they travel along the Pacific Flyway. Several wildlife refuges are in the immediate area, including two separate chunks of the Imperial Wildfowl Management Area, to the west and south, and the huge Wister Waterfowl Management Area, northwest of Niland. (For side-trip options, see the *Bombay Beach* listing in this chapter.)

Campsites, facilities: There are 40 sites for RVs or tents; some sites have partial hookups. Picnic tables, cabanas, and barbecue pits are provided. Restrooms with flush toilets and showers, a concession stand, beer, bait, fishing and hunting licenses, and a boat launch are available. The water at this park is not certified for drinking. Leashed pets are permitted.

Reservations, fees: Reservations are not ac-

cepted. Sites are $7–12 per night, $2 per night for each additional vehicle. Monthly rates available. Open year-round.

Directions: From Mecca, drive south on Highway 111 to Niland, and continue to Sinclair Road. Turn right and drive 3.5 miles to Garst Road. Turn right and drive 1.5 miles to the end of Garst Road at Red Hill Road. Turn left on Red Hill Road and drive to the park at the end of the road.

From El Centro, drive north on Highway 111 to Brawley and Highway 78/Main Street. Turn west (left) on Highway 78/Main Street and drive a short distance to Highway 111. Turn right (north) and drive to Calipatria. Continue north on Highway 111 just outside of Calipatria to Sinclair Road. Turn left on Sinclair Road and drive to Garst Road. Turn right and drive 1.5 miles to where it ends at Red Hill Road. Turn left at Red Hill Road and drive to the end of the road and the marina and the campground.

Contact: Red Hill Marina, tel./fax 760/348-2310.

75 WIEST LAKE COUNTY PARK

Scenic rating: 4

on Wiest Lake

This is a developed county park along the southern shore of Wiest Lake, which adjoins the Imperial Wildfowl Management Area to the north. Wiest Lake is just 50 acres, set 110 feet below sea level, and a prized area with such desolate country in the surrounding region. Waterskiing and sailboarding can be excellent, although few take advantage of the latter. Swimming is allowed when lifeguards are on duty. The lake is most popular for fishing, with trout planted in winter and catfish in summer. The lake also has bass and bluegill. The Salton Sea, about a 20-minute drive to the northwest, is a worthy side trip.

Campsites, facilities: There are 20 tent sites and 24 sites with full hookups (50 amps) for RVs up to 45 feet. Picnic tables and fire grills are provided. There is no drinking water. Restrooms with flush toilets and showers, a boat ramp, and a dump station are available. A store, coin laundry, and propane gas are available within five miles. Leashed pets are permitted.

Reservations, fees: Reservations are not accepted. Sites are $7–12 per night, $2 per night for each additional vehicle. Monthly rates available. Open year-round.

Directions: From El Centro, drive north on Highway 111 to Brawley and Highway 78/Main Street. Turn west (left) on Highway 78/Main Street and drive a short distance to Highway 111. Turn right (north) on Highway 111 and drive four miles to Rutherford Road (well signed). Turn right (east) and drive two miles to the park entrance on the right.

Contact: Wiest Lake County Park, tel./fax 760/344-3712.

76 CULP VALLEY PRIMITIVE CAMP AREA

Scenic rating: 4

near Peña Springs in Anza-Borrego Desert State Park

Culp Valley is set near Peña Springs, which is more of a mudhole than a spring. A 600-yard hike takes you to an overlook of Hellhole Canyon and an eastern view of the Borrego Valley. The elevation at this campground is 3,400 feet.

Campsites, facilities: This is a primitive, open camping area for tents or small RVs of any length (no hookups). Vault toilets are available. No drinking water is available. Fires are permitted in metal containers. Garbage and ashes must be packed out. Leashed pets are permitted in the campground, but not on trails.

Reservations, fees: Reservations are not ac-

cepted. There is no fee for camping. Open year-round.

Directions: From Julian, at the junction of Highway 78 and Highway 79, drive east on Highway 78 (steep and curvy) for 10 miles to Highway S2. Turn left (north) and drive 16 miles to Highway S22/Borrego Salton Seaway. Turn right (east) and drive 10 miles to the campground entrance road on the left.

Contact: Anza-Borrego Desert State Park, Visitor Center, 760/767-4205; Colorado Desert District, 760/767-5311, fax 760/767-7492, www.parks.ca.gov.

77 BORREGO PALM CANYON

Scenic rating: 4

in Anza-Borrego Desert State Park

This is one of the best camps in Anza-Borrego Desert State Park, with two excellent hikes available. The short hike into Borrego Palm Canyon is like being transported to another world, from the desert to the tropics, complete with a small waterfall, a rare sight in these parts. Panorama Overlook Trail also starts here. An excellent visitors center is available, offering an array of exhibits and a slide show. The elevation is 760 feet. Anza-Borrego Desert State Park is one of the largest state parks in the continental United States, covering more than 600,000 acres and with 500 miles of dirt roads. The park is appropriately named for the desert bighorn sheep (borrego in Spanish) that live in the mountains.

Campsites, facilities: There are 65 sites for tents or RVs up to 25 feet (no hookups), 52 sites with full hookups (30 amps) for RVs up to 35 feet, and five group tent sites for up to 24 people each. Picnic tables and fire grills are provided. Drinking water, restrooms with flush toilets and showers, and dump station are available. A store, coin laundry, and propane gas are nearby. Some facilities are wheelchair-accessible. Leashed pets are permitted.

Reservations, fees: Reservations are accepted at 800/444-PARK (800/444-7275) or www.recreation.gov ($7.50 reservation fee). Sites are $20–29 per night, $53 per night for group sites. Open year-round.

Directions: From Julian, at the junction of Highway 78 and Highway 79, drive east on Highway 78 (steep and curvy) for 19.5 miles to Yaqui Pass Road/County Road S3. Turn left (north) and drive eight miles to Borrego Springs and Palm Canyon Drive. Turn left (west) and drive 4.5 miles to the campground entrance road on the right.

Contact: Anza-Borrego Desert State Park, Visitor Center, 760/767-4205; Colorado Desert District, 760/767-5311, fax 760/767-7492, www.parks.ca.gov.

78 VERN WHITAKER HORSE CAMP

🏃 🐴 🚐 ⛺

Scenic rating: 5

in Anza-Borrego Desert State Park

This camp is popular during spring and fall, with lighter use during the winter. The 30 miles of horse trails attract equestrian campers. Campers are expected to clean up after their horses, and garbage bins are available for manure.

Campsites, facilities: There are 10 equestrian sites for tents or RVs up to 24 feet (no hookups). Picnic tables and fire grills are provided. Restrooms with flush toilets, an outdoor shower, drinking water, picnic areas, group gathering area, horse-washing station, and horse corrals are available. Leashed pets are permitted in the campground, but not on trails or in wilderness.

Reservations, fees: Reservations are accepted at 800/444-PARK (800/444-7275) or www.recreation.gov ($7.50 reservation fee). Sites are $20 per night, which includes two horses, $2 per additional horse per night. Open October through May.

Directions: From Julian, at the junction of Highway 78 and Highway 79, drive east on Highway 78 (steep and curvy) for 19.5 miles to Yaqui Pass Road/County Road 53. Turn left (north) and drive eight miles to Palm Canyon Drive. Turn left and drive to Borrego Springs and bear right (at the traffic circle) onto northbound Borrego Springs Road. Drive four miles on Borrego Springs Road to Henderson Canyon Road. Bear right and drive a short distance to the campground entrance road (look for the metal sign). Turn left and continue four miles to the camp. Note: Part of the last four miles are on a private road; please respect the property owner's rights.

Contact: Anza-Borrego Desert State Park, Visitor Center, 760/767-4205; Colorado Desert District, 760/767-5311, fax 760/767-7492, www.parks.ca.gov.

79 ARROYO SALADO PRIMITIVE CAMP AREA

🏃 🐴 🚐 ⛺

Scenic rating: 5

in Anza-Borrego Desert State Park

This camp is a primitive spot set along (and named after) an ephemeral stream, the Arroyo Salado. About eight miles to the west is the trailhead for Thimble Trail, which is routed south into a wash in the Borrego Badlands. The elevation is 880 feet.

Campsites, facilities: This is a primitive, open camping area for tents or small RVs of any length (no hookups). Vault toilets are available. No drinking water is available. Fires are allowed in metal containers. Garbage and ashes must be packed out. Open fires are not allowed. Leashed pets are permitted in the campground, but not on trails or in wilderness.

Reservations, fees: Reservations are not accepted. There is no fee for camping. Open year-round.

Directions: From Julian, at the junction of

Highway 78 (steep and curvy) and Highway 79, drive east on Highway 78 for 19.5 miles to Yaqui Pass Road/County Road S3. Turn left (north) and drive eight miles to Borrego Springs and Palm Canyon Drive. Turn right on Palm Canyon Drive (becomes Highway 522) and drive 20 miles (past Fonts Point) to the campground entrance on the right.

Contact: Anza-Borrego Desert State Park, Visitor Center, 760/767-4205; Colorado Desert District, 760/767-5311, fax 760/767-7492, www.parks.ca.gov.

80 YAQUI PASS PRIMITIVE CAMP AREA

Scenic rating: 1

in Anza-Borrego Desert State Park

This extremely primitive area is set beside rough Yaqui Pass Road at an elevation of 1,730 feet. The camping area is a large, open, sloping area of asphalt, where it is darn near impossible to get an RV level. The trailhead for Kenyon Loop Trail is to the immediate south. This spot is often overlooked because the Tamarisk Grove camp nearby provides shade, drinking water, and a feature trail.

Campsites, facilities: This is a primitive, open camping area for tents or small RVs of any length (no hookups). No drinking water or toilets are available. No open fires are allowed. Garbage must be packed out. Leashed pets are permitted, but not on trails or in wilderness.

Reservations, fees: No reservations are accepted and there are no fees. Open year-round.

Directions: From Julian, at the junction of Highway 78 and Highway 79, drive east on Highway 78 (steep and curvy) for 19.5 miles to Yaqui Pass Road/County Road S3. Turn left (north) and drive 2.5 miles to the campground entrance on the right. The access road is rough and the camping area has few level areas for large RVs, so only small RVs are recommended.

Contact: Anza-Borrego Desert State Park, Visitor Center, 760/767-4205; Colorado Desert District, 760/767-5311, fax 760/767-7492, www.parks.ca.gov.

81 YAQUI WELL PRIMITIVE CAMP AREA

Scenic rating: 2

in Anza-Borrego Desert State Park

This camp is used primarily as an overflow area if the more developed Tamarisk Grove camp is full. Cactus Loop Trail, a 2.5-mile loop hike that passes seven varieties of cacti, starts at Tamarisk Grove. The elevation is 1,400 feet.

Campsites, facilities: This is a primitive, open camping area for tents or small RVs of any length (no hookups). Vault toilets are available. No drinking water is available. Fires are permitted in metal containers. Garbage and ashes must be packed out. Open fires are not permitted. Leashed pets are permitted, but not on trails or in wilderness.

Reservations, fees: No reservations are accepted and there are no fees. Open year-round.

Directions: From Julian, at the junction of Highway 78 and Highway 79, drive east on Highway 78 (steep and curvy) for 19.5 miles to Yaqui Pass Road/County Road S3. Turn left (north) and drive a short distance to the campground entrance road on the left. The access road is rough and the camping area has few level areas for large RVs, so only small RVs are recommended.

Contact: Anza-Borrego Desert State Park, Visitor Center, 760/767-4205; Colorado Desert District, 760/767-5311, fax 760/767-7492, www.parks.ca.gov.

82 TAMARISK GROVE
👥 🐕 ♿ 🚐 ⛺

Scenic rating: 7

in Anza-Borrego Desert State Park

This is the number-one campground in Anza-Borrego Desert State Park, and it is easy to see why: Big tamarisk trees provide shade, and the park provides limited drinking water (recommended that you bring your own water as a backup). It is one of three camps in the immediate area, so if this camp is full, primitive Yaqui Well to the immediate west and Yaqui Pass to the north on Yaqui Pass Road provide alternatives. Cactus Loop Trail, with the trailhead just north of camp, provides a hiking option. This is a 1.5-mile loop that passes seven varieties of cacti, some as tall as people. The elevation is 1,400 feet at this campground.

Campsites, facilities: There are 27 sites for tents or RVs up to 21 feet (no hookups). Picnic tables and fire grills are provided. Restrooms with flush toilets and coin showers and limited drinking water are available. Some facilities are wheelchair-accessible. Leashed pets are permitted in the campground, but not on trails or in wilderness.

Reservations, fees: Reservations are accepted at www.reserveamerica.com ($7.50 reservation fee). Sites are $20 per night, $6 per night for each additional vehicle. Open October through May.

Directions: From Julian, at the junction of Highway 78 and Highway 79, drive east on Highway 78 (steep and curvy) for 19.5 miles to Yaqui Pass Road/County Road S3. Turn left (north) and drive 0.5 mile to the campground on the right.

Contact: Anza-Borrego Desert State Park, Visitor Center, 760/767-4205; Colorado Desert District, 760/767-5311, fax 760/767-7492, www.parks.ca.gov.

83 OCOTILLO WELLS STATE VEHICLE RECREATION AREA
👥 🚲 🏕 🚐 ⛺

Scenic rating: 4

in Ocotillo Wells

This can be a wild place, a giant OHV camp where the population of Ocotillo Wells can go from 10 to 5,000 overnight, no kidding. Yet if you arrive when there is no off-road event, it can also be a lonely, extremely remote destination. Some locals call the OHV crowd "escapees" and watch stunned as they arrive every February for two or three weeks. OHV events are held here occasionally as well. Mountain bikers also use these trails. One great side note is that annually there is "Desert Cleanup Day," when OHV users will clean up the place; date changes every year. The non-OHV crowd can still use this camp, but most come in the winter on weekdays, when activity is lower. The landscape is barren desert, dry as an iguana's back. A few shade ramadas are provided. The area covers 72,000 acres, ranging from below sea level to an elevation of 400 feet. It is adjacent to Anza-Borrego Desert State Park, another 600,000 acres of wildlands. The wash-and-ridge terrain includes a butte with dunes, a sand bowl, a blow sand dune, and springs. After wet winters, the blooms of wildflowers can be excellent. While this area is well known as a wild play area for the OHV crowd, it is also a place where on most days you can literally disappear and see no one. All drivers should watch for soft ground. Many vehicles get stuck here and have to be towed out. Also, dispersed camping is allowed in most of these state park lands.

Campsites, facilities: There are 60 dispersed primitive sites for tents or RVs of any length (no hookups). Picnic tables and fire rings are provided. Chemical toilets and shade ramadas are available. There is no drinking water. A coin-shower building is available near the ranger station, and another is 3.5 miles east at Holmes Camp. A store, restaurants, propane, and auto supplies are available four miles away in Ocotillo Wells. A gas station is seven miles from the ranger station. Leashed pets are permitted.

Reservations, fees: No reservations are accepted and there is no fee. This is a 30-day maximum stay per year. Open year-round.

Directions: From Julian, at the junction of Highway 78 and Highway 79, drive east on Highway 78 for 31.5 miles to Ranger Station Road. Turn left and drive 0.25 mile to the ranger station. (Note: For an alternate route, advisable for big rigs, that avoids curvy sections of Highway 78, see the detour route detailed in the *Stagecoach Trails* listing in this chapter.)

Contact: Ocotillo Wells SVRA, 760/767-5391, fax 760/767-4951, www.parks.ca.gov or www.ohv.parks.ca.gov.

84 FISH CREEK
🏃 🐕 ⛺

Scenic rating: 3

in Anza-Borrego Desert State Park

This primitive camp is set just inside the eastern border of Anza-Borrego Desert State Park at the foot of the Vallecito Mountains to the west. This is the closest camp to the Ocotillo Wells State Vehicular Recreation Area, which is 12 miles to the north. RVs are not recommended because of the steep access road. Note that the Elephant Tree Discovery Trail is a few miles north of camp.

Campsites, facilities: There are eight sites for tents. Vault toilets and Wi-Fi are available and some sites have picnic tables and fire rings. No drinking water is available. Garbage must be packed out. Leashed pets are permitted.

Reservations, fees: Reservations are not accepted. There is no fee for camping. Open year-round.

Directions: From Julian, at the junction of Highway 78 and Highway 79, drive east on

Highway 78 (steep and curvy) for 34 miles to Ocotillo Wells and Split Mountain Road. Turn right (south) and drive seven miles to the campground access road. Drive two miles to the campground entrance on the left.

Contact: Anza-Borrego Desert State Park, Visitor Center, 760/767-4205; Colorado Desert District, 760/767-5311, fax 760/767-7492, www.parks.ca.gov.

85 VALLECITO COUNTY PARK
🏠 🐕 🚐 ⛺

Scenic rating: 3

near Anza-Borrego Desert State Park

This county park in the desert gets little attention in the face of the other nearby attractions. This is a 71-acre park built around a sod reconstruction of the historic Vallecito Stage Station. It was part of the Butterfield Overland Stage from 1858 to 1861. The route carried mail and passengers from Missouri to San Francisco in 25 days, covering 2,800 miles. Vallecito means "little valley." It provides a quiet alternative to some of the busier campgrounds in the desert. One bonus is that it is usually 10 degrees cooler here than at Agua Caliente. A covered picnic area is a big plus. Other nearby destinations include Agua Caliente Hot Springs, Anza-Borrego Desert State Park to the east, and Lake Cuyamaca and Cuyamaca Rancho State Park about 35 miles away. The elevation is 1,500 feet.

Campsites, facilities: There are 44 sites for tents or RVs up to 40 feet (no hookups), one group area for up to 15 RVs, and one youth camping area for up to 35 people. Picnic tables, fire rings, and barbecues are provided. Drinking water, flush toilets, and a playground are available. Leashed pets are permitted.

Reservations, fees: Reservations are available at 877/565-3600 ($5 reservation fee). Sites are $15 per night, $100–200 per night for the group area, $25 per night for the youth group area, $1 per pet per night. Some credit cards accepted. Open Labor Day weekend through Memorial Day weekend; closed June, July, and August.

Directions: From El Cajon, drive east on I-8 for about 75 miles to the town of Ocotillo (the first town after crossing from San Diego County to Imperial County) and County Road S2/Imperial Highway. Turn north (left) on County Road S2/Imperial Highway and drive 30 miles to the park entrance.

Contact: San Diego County Parks Department, 858/694-3049, fax 858/495-5841, www.sdparks.org.

86 AGUA CALIENTE REGIONAL PARK

Scenic rating: 3

near Anza-Borrego Desert State Park

This is a popular park in winter. It has two naturally fed pools: A large outdoor thermal pool is kept at its natural 90°F, and an indoor pool is heated to 102°F and outfitted with jets. Everything is hot here. The weather is hot, the coffee is hot, and the water is hot. And hey, that's what "Agua Caliente" means— hot water, named after the nearby hot springs. Anza-Borrego Desert State Park is also nearby. If you would like to see some cold water, Lake Cuyamaca and Cuyamaca Rancho State Park are about 35 miles away. The elevation is 1,350 feet. The park covers 910 acres with several miles of hiking trails.

Campsites, facilities: There are 106 sites with full or partial hookups (30 amps) for RVs up to 40 feet, 35 sites with no hookups for tents or RVs, and a group area for up to 100 people. Picnic tables and fire grills are provided. Restrooms with flush toilets and showers, drinking water, outdoor and indoor pools, picnic area, and a playground with horseshoes and shuffleboard are available. Groceries and propane

gas are nearby. Some facilities are wheelchair-accessible. No pets are allowed.

Reservations, fees: Reservations are accepted at 877/565-3600 ($5 reservation fee). Sites are $15–25 per night, and the group area is $100–200 per night. Some credit cards accepted. Open Labor Day weekend through Memorial Day weekend; closed June, July, and August.

Directions: From El Cajon, drive east on I-8 about 75 miles to the town of Ocotillo (the first town after crossing from San Diego County to Imperial County) and County Road S2/Imperial Highway. Turn north (left) on County Road S2/Imperial Highway and drive 25 miles to the park entrance.

From Julian, take Highway 78 east and drive 12 miles to County Road S2/San Felipe Road. Turn right on County Road S2/San Felipe Road and drive 21 miles south to the park entrance.

Contact: San Diego County Parks Department, 858/694-3049, fax 858/495-5841, www.sdparks.org.

87 MOUNTAIN PALM SPRINGS PRIMITIVE CAMP AREA

Scenic rating: 4

in Anza-Borrego Desert State Park

A plus for this camping area is easy access from County Road S2, but no water is a giant minus. Regardless of pros and cons, only hikers will get the full benefit of the area. A trail leads south to Bow Willow Creek (and Bow Willow) and onward into Bow Willow Canyon. The Carrizo Badlands Overlook is on the southeast side of Sweeney Pass, about a 10-minute drive south on County Road S2. The elevation is 760 feet.

Campsites, facilities: This is a primitive, open camping area for tents or RVs of any length (no hookups). Vault toilets are available. No

CAMPING

drinking water is available. Fires are permitted in metal containers. Garbage and ashes must be packed out. Leashed pets are permitted, but not on trails or in wilderness.

Reservations, fees: Reservations are not accepted. There is no fee for camping. Open year-round.

Directions: From El Cajon, drive east on I-8 for about 75 miles to the town of Ocotillo (the first town after crossing from San Diego County to Imperial County) and County Road S2/Imperial Highway. Turn north (left) on County Road S2/Imperial Highway and drive 27.5 miles to the campground entrance road on the left (about 0.5 mile past the Bow Willow campground turnoff). Turn left and continue 0.75 mile to the camp.

Contact: Anza-Borrego Desert State Park, Visitor Center, 760/767-4205; Colorado Desert District, 760/767-5311, fax 760/767-7492, www.parks.ca.gov.

88 BOW WILLOW

Scenic rating: 4

near Bow Willow Canyon in Anza-Borrego Desert State Park

Bow Willow Canyon is a rugged setting that can be explored by hiking the trail that starts at this camp. A short distance east of the camp, the trail forks to the south to Rockhouse Canyon. For a good side trip, drive back to County Road S2 and head south over Sweeney Pass for the view at the Carrizo Badlands Overlook.

Campsites, facilities: There are 16 sites for tents or RVs up to 24 feet (no hookups). Picnic tables, fire rings, and shade ramadas are provided. Limited drinking water and vault toilets are available. Leashed pets are permitted in the campground, but not on trails.

Reservations, fees: Reservations are not accepted. Sites are $7 per night. Open year-round.

Directions: From El Cajon, drive east on I-8 about 75 miles to the town of Ocotillo (the first town after crossing from San Diego County to Imperial County) and County Road S2/Imperial Highway. Turn north (left) on County Road S2/Imperial Highway and drive 27 miles to the gravel campground entrance road on the left.

Contact: Anza-Borrego Desert State Park, Visitor Center, 760/767-4205; Colorado Desert District, 760/767-5311, fax 760/767-7492, www.parks.ca.gov.

89 RIO BEND RV AND GOLF RESORT

Scenic rating: 5

near El Centro

This resort is set at 50 feet below sea level near Mount Signal, about a 20-minute drive south of the Salton Sea. For some, this region is a godforsaken wasteland, but hey, that makes arriving at this park all the more like coming to a mirage in the desert. This resort is a combination RV park and year-round community with park models for sale. Management does what it can to offer visitors recreational options, including a nine-hole golf course. It's hot out here, sizzling most of the year, but dry and cool in the winter, the best time to visit.

Campsites, facilities: There are 500 sites for RVs of any length, including 460 pull-through sites with full hookups (30 and 50 amps). Group sites have partial hookups. Picnic tables are provided. Cable TV and restrooms with showers are available. Two small, stocked lakes for catch-and-release fishing, a convenience store, café, heated swimming pool, spa, shuffleboard, volleyball, horseshoes, bocce ball, pet park, nine-hole golf course, library, pool table, club room, organized activities, and modem access are available on a seasonal basis. Some facilities are wheelchair-accessible. A small store is nearby. Leashed pets are permitted.

Reservations, fees: Reservations are accepted.

Sites are $50 per night in winter, $38 per night in summer, $3 per person for more than two people. Weekly, monthly, and annual rates available. Some credit cards accepted. Open year-round.

Directions: From El Centro, drive west on I-8 for seven miles to the Drew Road exit. Take that exit and drive south on Drew Road for 0.25 mile to the park on the right (1589 Drew Road).

Contact: Rio Bend RV and Golf Resort, 760/352-7061 or 800/545-6481, www. riobend-rvgolfresort.com.

90 IMPERIAL SAND DUNES RECREATION AREA
🏃 🐕 🚐 ⛺

Scenic rating: 1

east of Brawley

Gecko, Roadrunner, and Midway campgrounds are three of the many camping options at Imperial Sand Dunes Recreation Area. There isn't a tree within a million miles of this camp. People who wind up here all have the same thing in common: They're ready to ride across the dunes in their dune buggies or off-highway vehicles. The dune season is on a weather-permitting basis. Note that several areas are off-limits to motorized vehicles and camping because of plant and habitat protection; hiking in these areas is allowed. There are opportunities for hiking on this incredible moonscape. Other recreation options include watching the sky and waiting for a cloud to show up. A gecko, by the way, is a harmless little lizard. I've had them crawl on the sides of my tent. Nice little fellows.

Campsites, facilities: There are numerous dispersed sites for tents or RVs of any length (no hookups). Vault toilets and a trash bin are available. No drinking water is available. A few sites have camping pads. Leashed pets are permitted.

Reservations, fees: Reservations are not ac-

cepted. Sites are $25 per week, $90 per season, if purchased from the vendor. Permits purchased onsite cost $40 per week, $120 per season, with a 14-day stay limit every 28 days. Open year-round.

Directions: From Brawley, drive east on Highway 78 for 27 miles to Gecko Road. Turn south on Gecko Road and drive three miles to the campground entrance on the left. To reach Roadrunner Camp, continue for two miles to the campground at the end of the road.

Contact: Bureau of Land Management, El Centro Field Office, 760/337-4400, fax 760/337-4490. For more information on closed areas, contact the Imperial Sand Dunes ranger station at 760/344-4400.

91 PICACHO STATE RECREATION AREA
🏃 🏖 🚣 🛥 🐕 ♿ 🚐 ⛺

Scenic rating: 6

near Taylor Lake on the Colorado River

To get here, you really have to want it. Picacho State Recreation Area is way out there, requiring a long drive north out of Winterhaven on a spindly little road. The camp is on the southern side of Taylor Lake on the Colorado River. The park is the best deal around for many miles, though, with boat ramps, waterskiing, good bass fishing, and, occasionally, crazy folks having the time of their lives. The sun and water make a good combination. This recreation area includes eight miles of the lower Colorado River. Park wildlife includes wild burros and bighorn sheep, with thousands of migratory waterfowl on the Pacific Flyway occasionally taking up residence. More than 100 years ago, Picacho was a gold-mining town with a population of 2,500 people. Visitors should always carry extra water and essential supplies.

Campsites, facilities: There are 58 sites for tents or RVs up to 35 feet (no hookups), two group sites for up to 100 people, and two boat-in campsites. Picnic tables and fire grills are provided. Drinking water, pit toilets, dump station, solar showers, and two boat launches are available. Some facilities are wheelchair-accessible. Leashed pets are permitted.

Reservations, fees: Reservations are accepted for group sites only at 760/996-2963. Sites are $10 per night. Group sites are $37 per night for up to 12 vehicles. Boat-in group sites are $45 per night for up to 15 people, and $3 per person per night for additional people. Open year-round.

Directions: From El Centro, drive east on I-8 to Winterhaven and the exit for Winterhaven/4th Avenue. Take that exit to Winterhaven Drive. Turn left on Winterhaven Drive and drive 0.5 mile to County Road S24/Picacho Road. Turn right and drive 24 miles (crossing rail tracks, driving under a railroad bridge, and over the American Canal, the road becoming dirt for the last 18 miles) to the campground. The road is not suitable for large RVs. The drive takes 1–2 hours from Winterhaven. In summer, thunderstorms can cause flash flooding, making short sections of the road impassable.

Contact: Picacho State Recreation Area, c/o Salton Sea State Recreation Area, 760/996-2963 (reservations), www.parks.ca.gov.

92 SQUAW LAKE
🏃 🏊 🛶 🎣 🛖 🐕 ♿ 🚐 ⛺

Scenic rating: 6

near the Colorado River

Take your pick. There are two camps near the Colorado River in this area (the other is Senator Wash). This one is near Squaw Lake, created by the nearby Imperial Dam on the Colorado River. These sites provides opportunities for swimming, fishing, boating, and hiking, featuring direct boat access to the Colorado River. Wildlife includes numerous waterfowl, as well as quail, coyotes, and reptiles. A speed limit of 5 mph is enforced on the lake; no wakes permitted. The no-wake zone ends at the Colorado River.

Campsites, facilities: There are 125 sites for RVs of any length (no hookups) and dispersed sites for tents. Picnic tables and barbecue grills are provided. Four restrooms with flush toilets and outdoor showers are available. Drinking water is available at a central location. Two boat ramps are nearby. Some facilities are wheelchair-accessible. Leashed pets are permitted.

Reservations, fees: Reservations are not accepted. Sites are $15 per night. There is a year-round maximum 14-day limit for every 28 days. Open year-round.

Directions: Drive on I-8 to Yuma, Arizona, and the exit for 4th Avenue. Take that exit and drive to Imperial Highway/County Road S24. Turn north and drive 22 miles to Senator Wash Road. Turn left and drive about four miles (well signed) to the lake and campground on the right.

Contact: Bureau of Land Management, Yuma Field Office, 928/317-3200, fax 928/317-3250.

93 SENATOR WASH RECREATION AREA
🏊 🛶 🎣 🛖 ♿ 🚐 ⛺

Scenic rating: 6

near Senator Wash Reservoir

Senator Wash Reservoir Recreation Area features two campgrounds, named (surprise) Senator Wash South Shore and Senator Wash North Shore. This recreation area is approximately 50 acres, with many trees of various types and several secluded camping areas. At Senator Wash North Shore (where there are fewer facilities than at South Shore), campsites are both on the water as well as further inland. Gravel beaches provide access to the reservoir. Boat ramps are nearby. This spot provides boating, fishing, OHV riding, wildlife-viewing, and opportunities for solitude and sightseeing.

Campsites, facilities: There are numerous dispersed sites for tents or RVs of any length (no hookups). No drinking water is available. At South Shore, there are restrooms with flush toilets, outdoor showers, and drinking water. A buoyed swimming area and boat ramp providing boat-in access to campsites at North Shore is available about 0.25 mile from South Shore. At North Shore, there are two vault toilets, but no drinking water; boat ramp is approximately 0.25 mile away. Some facilities are wheelchair-accessible. No camping at the boat ramp. Leashed pets are permitted.

Reservations, fees: Reservations are not accepted. Sites are $15 per night. There is a year-round maximum 14-day limit for every 28 days. Open year-round.

Directions: Drive on I-8 to Yuma, Arizona, and the exit for 4th Avenue. Take that exit and drive to Imperial Highway/County Road S24. Turn north and drive 22 miles to Senator Wash Road. Turn left and drive about three miles south to Mesa Campground. Turn left and drive 200 yards to the South Shore Campground access road on the right. Turn right and drive to the reservoir and campground.

Contact: Bureau of Land Management, Yuma Field Office, 928/317-3200, fax 928/317-3250.

94 MIDWAY

Scenic rating: 6

in the Imperial Sand Dunes Recreation Area

This is off-highway-vehicle headquarters, a place where people bring their three-wheelers, four-wheelers, and motorcycles. That's because a large area has been set aside just for this type of recreation. Good news is that this area has become more family-oriented because of increased enforcement, eliminating much of the lawlessness and lunatic behavior of the past. As you drive in, you will enter the Buttercup Recreation Area, which is part of the Imperial Sand Dunes Recreation Area. You camp almost anywhere you like, and nobody beefs. Note that several areas are off-limits to motorized vehicles and camping because of plant and habitat protection; hiking in these areas is allowed. (See the *Imperial Sand Dunes Recreation Area* listing in this chapter for more options.)

Campsites, facilities: There are several primitive sites for tents or RVs of any length (no hookups). Vault toilets and a trash bin are available. No drinking water is available. Leashed pets are permitted.

Reservations, fees: Reservations are not accepted. Sites are $25 per week, $90 per season. Permits purchased onsite cost $40 per week, $120 per season. Open year-round, weather permitting.

Directions: From El Centro, drive east on I-8 for about 40 miles to Gray's Wells Road (signed Sand Dunes). Take that exit and drive (it bears to the right) to a stop sign. Continue straight on Gray's Wells Road and drive three miles to another stop sign. To reach Buttercup Recreation Area, turn left and drive a short distance. To reach Midway, continue straight on Gray's Wells Road for 1.5 miles (the road turns from pavement to dirt and then dead-ends); camping is permitted anywhere in this region.

Contact: Bureau of Land Management, El Centro Field Office, 760/337-4400, fax 760/337-4490. For more information on closed areas, contact the Imperial Sand Dunes ranger station at 760/344-4400.

8529.

CALIFORNIA DESERTS HIKING

© ANN MARIE BROWN

BEST HIKES

The California deserts encompass a series of

state and regional parks located in the Mojave and Colorado Deserts. These include two of California's most spectacular national parks –Joshua Tree and Death Valley – plus Mojave National Preserve, the world-famous oasis of Palm Springs, and Anza-Borrego Desert State Park, California's largest state park. The trails in Vasquez Rocks, Saddleback Butte, Red Rock Canyon, and other nearby parks show off red-colored desert cliffs, tilted sandstone slabs, grassy knolls covered with California poppies, and forests of Joshua trees.

Joshua Tree is best known for its wide desert plains covered with strange-looking Joshua trees, amazing rock formations and boulder piles, rugged mountains, and gold-mining ruins. The park is situated where the high Mojave Desert meets the low Colorado Desert, producing a wide variety of desert flora. Much of the park is higher than 4,000 feet in elevation. The most comfortable weather usually occurs from October to May; summer temperatures frequently soar past 100 degrees. Hiking trails in Joshua Tree are plentiful and varied; destinations include gold-mine stamp mills, old homesteads, mountain summits, and fan palm oases.

Only 50 miles to the north, Mojave National Preserve is where the Mojave, Great Basin, and Sonoran Deserts join. As a result of this convergence, the Mojave contains a wide diversity of plant and animal life, as well as interesting geological features. Hiking trails lead to the summit of Cima Dome, a granite batholith covered with a dense forest of Joshua trees, and through the volcanic rock cliffs of Hole-in-the-Wall. The 500-foot-tall Kelso Dunes, second highest in California, are another of the preserve's attractions. No official trails lead to the top of the dunes because of the constantly swirling desert sands; hikers simply pick a route and start climbing.

Death Valley is home to the lowest point in elevation in the Western hemisphere: Badwater, at 282 feet below sea level. In stark contrast, it's also home to Telescope Peak, elevation 11,048 feet, which is snow-covered six months of the year. With a little effort, hikers can set foot in both places in the same day. In between these extremes are a wide range of ecological communities, from desert scrub to piñon and juniper woodlands. More than 900 plant species and 50 mammal species live in Death Valley. Hikers can choose from an amazing diversity of trails that lead to destinations such as 700-foot-high sand dunes, colorful badlands, towering rock walls, volcanic craters, old mining ruins, and even a waterfall in the desert.

The desert oasis of Palm Springs was originally the home of the Agua Caliente band of the Cahuilla Indians, who still own major portions of the town's land. Not unlike today's Palm Springs visitors, the Agua Caliente worshipped the pure water flowing down the desert canyons, the natural hot springs, and the wind-sheltering curve of the San Jacinto Mountains. Hikers should pay a visit to the Agua Caliente Indian Canyons for a real taste of the Palm Springs desert. You won't find manicured golf courses or trendy nightclubs in the Indian Canyons, but you will find lush stands of palms, mesquite, and creosote, as well as the magical silence of the desert.

Anza-Borrego Desert State Park encompasses 600,000 acres of palm groves, year-round creeks, slot canyons, and badlands. It is California's largest state park and more than three times the size of Zion National Park. Desert flora runs the gamut from the expected, like barrel cactus and mesquite, to the rare: stands of jumping cholla cactus and aptly named elephant trees. Majestic and endangered bighorn sheep are commonly seen. Hiking trails lead to leafy fan palm groves, cholla cactus gardens, and old homesteading sites. Hikers who show up in spring are treated to an array of desert wildflowers, including the distinctive flaming-red plumes of ocotillos.

Connoisseurs of barrel cactus, Joshua trees, palm groves, and other desert flora will find those treasures here in the California deserts. Come armed with a big hat and a plentiful supply of water, and you can help yourself to an abundance of options for desert hiking.

HIKING

HIKING

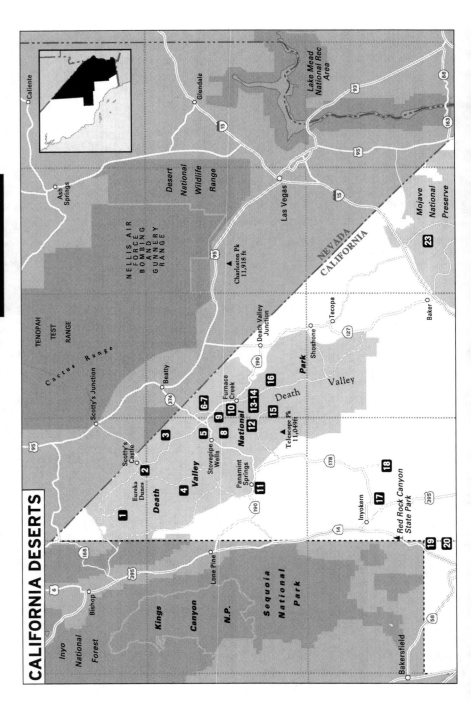

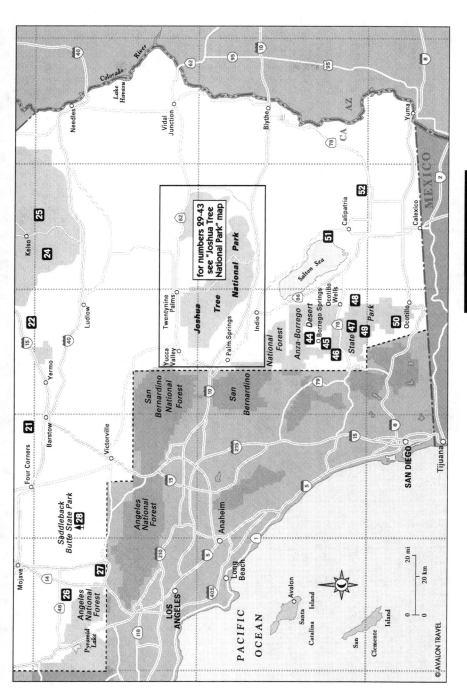

HIKING

HIKING

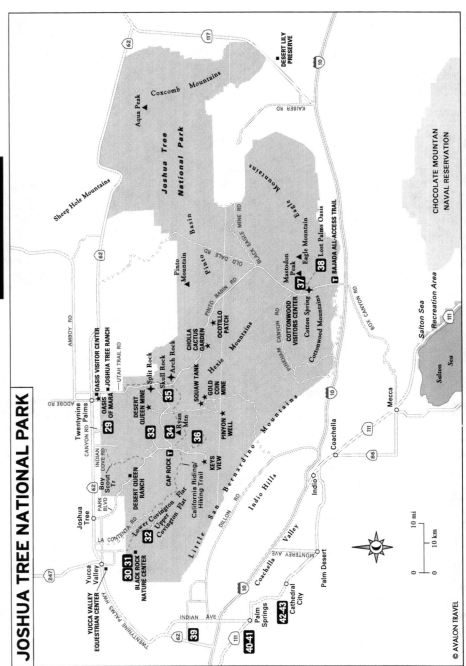

1 EUREKA DUNES
2.0 mi / 1.0 hr   🏃3 ⛰10

in Death Valley National Park north of Scotty's
Castle

It takes a heck of a lot of time and patience to drive to Eureka Dunes, but as soon as you see those giant icons of the desert, you'll know why you came. Eureka Dunes are the tallest sand dunes in California, and arguably also the tallest in North America. They rise nearly 700 feet from their base, creating a sandy, miniature mountain range that is home to several rare and endangered desert plants. Simply put, Eureka Dunes are a must-see in Death Valley. Hike to the top and snap a few pictures, and you'll go home with many weird and wonderful photographs of wind patterns on sand or your hiking partner traversing swirling dune ridge tops. From the trailhead, simply head for the clearly visible dunes. Because of the continually shifting desert sand, there is no marked trail, so make your own path. Your best bet is to climb to the top of the tallest dune you can find, then trace a ridgeline path from dune to dune. It's a strange, wonderful feeling to walk on the silky-soft sand crystals. And as you might expect, climbing the dunes is a slow proposition—take two steps forward, slide one step back, then repeat the process. Just take your time and enjoy the uniqueness of the experience. Also, be extremely careful not to step on any of the fragile dune vegetation—the Eureka Dunes are home to three different rare and endangered plants.

A few tips: Prepare yourself mentally and physically for the long drive to the trailhead (especially the bumpy 44-mile section on dirt roads), and you'll be far more likely to enjoy the trip. Take plenty of water and snacks with you for a long day. And most important: Attempt this adventure only when temperatures are cool in Death Valley.

User Groups: Hikers only. No dogs, horses, or mountain bikes. No wheelchair facilities.

Permits: No permits are required. There is a $20 entrance fee per vehicle at Death Valley National Park, good for seven days.

Maps: Free park maps are available at park entrance stations or by contacting Death Valley National Park at the address below. A more detailed map is available from Tom Harrison Maps. For a topographic map, ask the USGS for Last Chance Range Southwest.

Directions: From the Furnace Creek Visitors Center in Death Valley National Park, drive north on Highway 190 for 17 miles, then bear right on Scotty's Castle Road. In 32 miles you will pass the Grapevine entrance station. Continue northwest for three miles (keep left; don't bear right for Scotty's Castle) to the dirt road on the right signed for Eureka Dunes. (If you reach Ubehebe Crater, you've passed the dirt road.) Turn right and drive 44 miles to the Eureka Dunes parking area. A high-clearance vehicle is recommended; call to check on road conditions before heading out.

Contact: Death Valley National Park, P.O. Box 579, Death Valley, CA 92328, 760/786-3200, www.nps.gov/deva.

2 UBEHEBE AND LITTLE HEBE CRATER TRAIL
1.0 mi / 0.5 hr   🏃1 ⛰9

in Death Valley National Park near Scotty's
Castle

A walk along the rim of a not-so-ancient volcano is what you get on Little Hebe Crater Trail. The trail leads along Ubehebe Crater's southwest rim to Little Hebe and several older craters. Ubehebe Crater is 500 feet deep and 0.5 mile across, and was formed by volcanic activity that occurred between 300 and 1,000 years ago. Little Hebe and the other craters are much smaller but similar in appearance—mostly black and ash colored, with eroded walls that reveal a colorful blend of orange and rust from the minerals in the rock. At 0.5 mile from the trailhead, you reach a junction where you can continue straight ahead to Little Hebe Crater or just loop all the way around Ubehebe's rim. Take your pick—from the high rim of Ubehebe, it's easy to see where you're going, as well as down into the valley below, and far off to the Last Chance Range. Note that the trail surface is a mix of loose gravel and cinders, so it's a good idea to bring hiking boots or high-top shoes. A side note: Most visitors to Ubehebe Crater don't even bother with this trail. Instead, they just get out of their cars, make a beeline run for the bottom of the huge crater, and then moan and groan when they realize they have to make the steep climb back up. Go figure.

User Groups: Hikers only. No dogs, horses, or mountain bikes. No wheelchair facilities.

Permits: No permits are required. There is a $20 entrance fee per vehicle at Death Valley National Park, good for seven days.

Maps: Free park maps are available at park entrance stations or by contacting Death Valley National Park at the address below. A more detailed map is available from Tom Harrison Maps. For a topographic map, ask the USGS for Ubehebe Crater.

Directions: From the Furnace Creek Visitors Center in Death Valley National Park, drive north on Highway 190 for 17 miles, then bear right on Scotty's Castle Road. In 32 miles you will pass the Grapevine entrance station. Continue northwest for five miles to the left turnoff to Ubehebe Crater.

Contact: Death Valley National Park, P.O. Box 579, Death Valley, CA 92328, 760/786-3200, www.nps.gov/deva.

❸ FALL CANYON
5.6 mi / 3.0 hr

In Death Valley National Park near Scotty's Castle

Most park visitors take the one-way drive through Titus Canyon to see a desert canyon with giant alluvial fans and towering rock walls. But if you want to witness a similarly imposing desert scene on foot, take a hike in Titus Canyon's next-door neighbor, Fall Canyon. There is no formal trail, but the canyon walls keep you funneled in the right direction. From the parking area, hike to your left (north) on the unsigned trail. In 0.5 mile, you'll reach a wash, but its walls quickly narrow, then later widen again, then repeat the process. A gravel surface makes the walking a bit strenuous. Scan the walls' colorful surfaces as you walk, and you'll notice tiny arch formations and miniature caves and alcoves. At 2.8 miles, you are faced with a 20-foot dry fall, and this is where most hikers turn back. If you are experienced at rock scrambling, however, you can locate and follow a use trail on the canyon's south side to bypass the fall. After doing so, you'll enter a 0.5-mile-long, polished narrows area, which many consider to be as beautiful as the narrows in Death Valley's Mosaic Canyon.

User Groups: Hikers only. No dogs, horses, or mountain bikes. No wheelchair facilities.

Permits: No permits are required. There is a $20 entrance fee per vehicle at Death Valley National Park, good for seven days.

Maps: Free park maps are available at park entrance stations or by contacting Death Valley National Park at the address below. A more detailed map is available from Tom Harrison Maps. For a topographic map, ask the USGS for Ubehebe Crater.

Directions: From the Furnace Creek Visitors Center in Death Valley National Park, drive north on Highway 190 for 17 miles, then bear right on Scotty's Castle Road. In 14 miles, turn right at the sign for Titus Canyon. Drive 2.7 miles to the parking area, just before Titus Canyon Road becomes a one-way road. Begin hiking to the left of Titus Canyon on a narrow, unsigned trail heading north.

Contact: Death Valley National Park, P.O. Box 579, Death Valley, CA 92328, 760/786-3200, www.nps.gov/deva.

4 UBEHEBE PEAK

6.0 mi / 3.0 hr   🏃4 ⛰9

in Death Valley National Park

Are you prepared for a long drive and then a difficult hike? If you are, the rewards on this trip are great. The climb to Ubehebe Peak would be strenuous enough if you just accounted for the steep grade, but add in the fact that this is Death Valley, and the hike becomes a butt-kicker. The peak offers tremendous views of both the snowy Sierra Nevada and the desertlike Last Chance Range, as well as Racetrack and Saline Valleys. The trail is a narrow miners' route that switchbacks up and up and up, and you can be darn sure that you won't come across any shade on the way. There is no trail for the final 0.5 mile to the summit; most hikers content themselves with the view from the saddle below. (If you stop there, you won't miss out. The view is incredible, especially of the Grandstand rock formation far below, and the salt flats of the Saline Valley to the west.) Experienced climbers can make the final summit scramble. Total elevation gain is 1,900 feet; the summit is at 5,678 feet in elevation. Note: Before or after your trip, be sure to explore around the Racetrack area, where you can see the tracks of rocks that have slid along the surface of the mudflats, pushed by strong winds. To see them, drive about two miles south of this trailhead to the pullout and interpretive sign for the sliding rocks, then walk about a half mile out on the playa. Many a fine photograph has been shot of these fascinating rock tracks.

User Groups: Hikers only. No dogs, horses, or mountain bikes. No wheelchair facilities.

Permits: No permits are required. There is a $20 entrance fee per vehicle at Death Valley National Park, good for seven days.

Maps: Free park maps are available at park entrance stations or by contacting Death Valley National Park at the address below. A more detailed map is available from Tom Harrison Maps. For a topographic map, ask the USGS for Ubehebe Peak.

Directions: From the Furnace Creek Visitors Center in Death Valley National Park, drive north on Highway 190 for 17 miles, then bear right on Scotty's Castle Road. In 32 miles, you will pass the Grapevine entrance station, then continue northwest for 5.8 miles (keep left; don't bear right for Scotty's Castle). Turn right on the dirt road signed for Racetrack. Drive 20 miles on Racetrack Road. Bear right at Teakettle Junction and drive 5.9 miles to a pullout on the right side of the road, across from the large rock formation called the Grandstand. High-clearance vehicles are necessary on Racetrack Road.

Contact: Death Valley National Park, P.O. Box 579, Death Valley, CA 92328, 760/786-3200, www.nps.gov/deva.

5 MESQUITE FLAT SAND DUNES

3.0 mi / 1.0 hr   🏃1 ⛰8

in Death Valley National Park near Stovepipe Wells

Nothing makes a better introduction to Death Valley than a visit to the 80-foot-high Mesquite Flat sand dunes, near Stovepipe Wells. No, these aren't the giant sand dunes that Death Valley is famous for; those are the Eureka Dunes. But if you've just driven into the park, this hike will convince your senses that you're really in Death Valley, a place like no place else. There is no marked trail because of the continually shifting desert sands, so you just make a beeline from the roadside parking area to the dunes. How far you wander is completely up to you. Early in the morning or right about sunset are the best times to visit because of the incredible show of color and light in the ghostlike dunes. Full-moon nights are also popular, and it's easy to imagine why. They'll have you dreaming of Arabian nights. Note that there used to be another trailhead for these dunes off Scotty's Castle Road, but the access road has been closed. Now everybody heads to the dunes directly from Highway 190.

User Groups: Hikers only. No dogs, horses, or mountain bikes. No wheelchair facilities.

Permits: No permits are required. There is a $20 entrance fee per vehicle at Death Valley National Park, good for seven days.

Maps: Free park maps are available at park entrance stations or by contacting Death Valley National Park at the address below. A more detailed map is available from Tom Harrison Maps. For a topographic map, ask the USGS for Stovepipe Wells.

Directions: From Lone Pine on U.S. 395, drive east on Highway 136 for 18 miles. Continue east on Highway 190 for approximately 62 miles, past Stovepipe Wells Village, to the pullouts alongside the road near the sand dunes (exactly 2.2 miles east of Stovepipe Wells). Park alongside the road.

Contact: Death Valley National Park, P.O. Box 579, Death Valley, CA 92328, 760/786-3200, www.nps.gov/deva.

6 KEANE WONDER MINE TRAIL
3.2 mi / 2.0 hr 🏃4 ⛰️9

in Death Valley National Park

You wouldn't think a three-mile round-trip trail could be this hard. But then again, most people don't usually climb 1,600 feet in 1.5 miles, and especially not this close to sea level, in the desert. The million-dollar vistas on Keane Wonder Mine Trail are worth the trek, though, and they're sure to pay off at least as well as the Wonder gold and silver mine did in the early 20th century. The mine had such promise, in fact, that ambitious miners built an aerial tramway to carry loads of rock down the mountainside to the mill. The vein of ore ran dry in 1915, but the mine's mill and tramway ruins still exist, and you'll see them

on this steep trek into the Funeral Mountains. After only 0.5 mile of climbing, the views of Death Valley open wide; meanwhile, the path steepens and continues straight upward. When you pass mine shafts along the trail, remember to stay out of them; their list of hazards is long. The vistas, on the other hand, are perfectly safe and yours for the taking.

User Groups: Hikers only. No dogs, horses, or mountain bikes. No wheelchair facilities.

Permits: No permits are required. There is a $20 entrance fee per vehicle at Death Valley National Park, good for seven days.

Maps: Free park maps are available at park entrance stations or by contacting Death Valley National Park at the address below. A more detailed map is available from Tom Harrison Maps. For a topographic map, ask the USGS for Chloride City.

Directions: From the Furnace Creek Visitors Center in Death Valley National Park, drive 10 miles north on Highway 190 to the Beatty Cutoff Road. Bear right (north) on Beatty Cutoff Road and drive 5.7 miles to the right turnoff for Keane Wonder Mine. Turn right and drive 2.8 miles on a rough dirt road to the parking area.

Contact: Death Valley National Park, P.O. Box 579, Death Valley, CA 92328, 760/786-3200, www.nps.gov/deva.

7 KEANE WONDER SPRING
2.0 mi / 1.0 hr 🏃1 ⛰️7i

n Death Valley National Park

If you aren't up for the steep climb to the top of the tramway at Keane Wonder Mine (see previous listing), this easy and flat trail to Keane Wonder Spring provides a pleasant alternative. The mineral spring once provided water for the mining operation; now it provides a gathering place for birds and wildlife. Walk from the trailhead toward the large metal water tank to find the trail (on its left side). Follow an old pipeline northward along the base of the mountains, cross a wash, and pass mounds of travertine (a marblelike rock formed by the sulfur-rich springwater). The spring is just slightly off the trail 0.75 mile from the trailhead and not really worth the scramble required to access it. (It's a hole in the ground that reeks of hydrogen sulfide.) Instead, continue another 0.25 mile beyond the spring to the remains of an old stamp mill and cabin.

User Groups: Hikers only. No dogs, horses, or mountain bikes. No wheelchair facilities.

Permits: No permits are required. There is a $20 entrance fee per vehicle at Death Valley National Park, good for seven days.

Maps: Free park maps are available at park entrance stations or by contacting Death Valley National Park at the address below. A more detailed map is available from Tom Harrison Maps. For a topographic map, ask the USGS for Chloride City.

Directions: From the Furnace Creek Visitors Center in Death Valley National Park, drive 10 miles north on Highway 190 to the Beatty Cutoff Road. Bear right (north) on Beatty Cutoff Road and drive 5.7 miles to the turnoff for Keane Wonder Mine. Turn right and drive 2.8 miles on a rough dirt road to the parking area.

Contact: Death Valley National Park, P.O. Box 579, Death Valley, CA 92328, 760/786-3200, www.nps.gov/deva.

8 MOSAIC CANYON
1.0 mi / 0.5 hr   1 10

in Death Valley National Park near Stovepipe Wells

BEST (

The Mosaic Canyon hike is one of the scenic highlights of Death Valley, and it's accessible to all levels of hikers. The trail shows off plenty of colorful slickrock and polished marble as it winds its way up a narrow, high-walled canyon, which was formed by a fault zone. A rock formation called mosaic breccia—

multicolored rock fragments that appear to be cemented together—is embedded in the canyon walls. The best mosaics are visible in the first 0.25 mile, making this trip rewarding even for those who don't like to hike more than a short distance.

From the trailhead, the route enters the canyon almost immediately, and the smooth marble walls close in around you. At various points, the fissure you're walking through opens wider into "rooms" bordered by marble walls, then narrows again. After 0.3 mile, the canyon walls open out to a wide alluvial fan that is not quite as interesting as the narrows area. Many people turn around here, but if you like, you can continue walking another 1.5 miles. The path ends at a dry waterfall that is too high to be scaled.

User Groups: Hikers only. No dogs, horses, or mountain bikes. No wheelchair facilities.

Permits: No permits are required. There is a $20 entrance fee per vehicle at Death Valley National Park, good for seven days.

Maps: Free park maps are available at park entrance stations or by contacting Death Valley National Park at the address below. A more detailed map is available from Tom Harrison Maps. For a topographic map, ask the USGS for Stovepipe Wells.

Directions: From Lone Pine on U.S. 395, drive east on Highway 136 for 18 miles. Continue east on Highway 190 for approximately 60 miles to 0.25 mile west of Stovepipe Wells Village. Look for the Mosaic Canyon turnoff, on the right. If you reach Stovepipe Wells Village, you missed the turnoff. Turn right and drive 2.2 miles to the trailhead parking lot. The last two miles are rough dirt road but are usually passable by passenger cars.

Contact: Death Valley National Park, P.O. Box 579, Death Valley, CA 92328, 760/786-3200, www.nps.gov/deva.

HIKING

HIKING

9 SALT CREEK INTERPRETIVE TRAIL

1.0 mi / 0.5 hr   🏃1 △8

in Death Valley National Park

BEST (

Salt Creek is exactly what its name implies—a stream of saline water—and it's home to the Salt Creek pupfish, a species that lives nowhere else. The fish underwent an incredible evolutionary change in order to live in this saline creek, which was once a part of a much larger freshwater lake. The biological alteration would be roughly the same as if humans decided to drink gasoline instead of water. In the spring (usually late February and March), you can look down into Salt Creek and spot the minnow-sized pupfish swimming about. The plants along the stream are typical of California coastal wetlands—salt grass and pickleweed. Birds congregate by the stream, including great blue herons. Because the trail is on a wooden boardwalk, it is accessible to all hikers, including wheelchair users.

User Groups: Hikers and wheelchairs. No dogs, horses, or mountain bikes.

Permits: No permits are required. There is a $20 entrance fee per vehicle at Death Valley National Park, good for seven days.

Maps: Interpretive trail brochures are available at park visitors centers or at the trailhead. Free park maps are available at park entrance stations or by contacting Death Valley National Park at the address below. A more detailed map is available from Tom Harrison Maps. For a topographic map, ask the USGS for Beatty Junction.

Directions: From the Furnace Creek Visitors Center in Death Valley National Park, drive 12 miles north on Highway 190 to the turnoff for Salt Creek. Turn left and drive one mile to the Salt Creek parking area.

Contact: Death Valley National Park, P.O. Box 579, Death Valley, CA 92328, 760/786-3200, www.nps.gov/deva.

10 HARMONY BORAX WORKS AND BORAX FLATS

1.0 mi / 0.5 hr   🏃1 △8

in Death Valley National Park

A stroll on Harmony Borax Works Interpretive Trail, combined with a longer excursion on neighboring Borax Flats, makes an easy and interesting walk through Death Valley's history. Borax was first discovered in Death Valley in 1881, but transporting it proved difficult, because the nearest railroad was 165 miles away, in Mojave, over fierce, rugged terrain. Enterprising miners figured out the solution: Build specially designed wagons that could carry huge, extra-heavy loads pulled by teams of 20 mules. The rest, as they say, is history. The paved loop leads past examples of the 20-mule team wagons, as well as equipment used for refining borax. At the west end of the loop, you can leave the pavement and walk out to the site where Chinese laborers gathered the stuff from the salt flats. The flats are easy to walk on, with a crusty, hard surface. Eventually the trail dissipates in the mud, so when your curiosity is satisfied, just turn around and head back.

User Groups: Hikers only. No dogs, horses, or mountain bikes. No wheelchair facilities.

Permits: No permits are required. There is a $20 entrance fee per vehicle at Death Valley National Park, good for seven days.

Maps: Free park maps are available at park entrance stations or by contacting Death Valley National Park at the address below. A more detailed map is available from Tom Harrison Maps. For a topographic map, ask the USGS for Furnace Creek.

Directions: From the Furnace Creek Visitors Center in Death Valley National Park, drive north on Highway 190 for 1.3 miles to the left turnoff for Harmony Borax Works and Mustard Canyon. Turn left, then stay to the left to reach the trailhead parking area.

Contact: Death Valley National Park, P.O.

Box 579, Death Valley, CA 92328, 760/786-3200, www.nps.gov/deva.

11 DARWIN FALLS
2.2 mi / 1.0 hr   🥾1 △8

in Death Valley National Park near Panamint Springs

Darwin Falls is a must-do desert hike. A waterfall in the desert is a rare and precious thing, a miracle of life in a harsh world. The trip is easy enough for young children, and although the temperatures in this area can be extreme in the summer, an early-morning start makes the short hike manageable almost year-round. Of course, be sure to carry water with you. Follow the trail into the canyon, and you'll soon see a trickle of water on the ground that grows wider and more substantial the farther you walk. You simply follow the stream, crossing it a few times, for about a mile. The canyon walls narrow, and the vegetation becomes much more lush. Just beyond a small stream-gauging station, you come to the waterfall—a 30-foot cascade tucked into a box canyon. A large cottonwood tree grows at its lip. In the spring, more than 80 species of resident and migrating birds have been sighted in this canyon.

User Groups: Hikers only. No dogs, horses, or mountain bikes. No wheelchair facilities.

Permits: No permits are required. Parking and access are free.

Maps: Free park maps are available at park entrance stations or by contacting Death Valley National Park at the address below. A more detailed map is available from Tom Harrison Maps. For a topographic map, ask the USGS for Panamint Springs.

Directions: From Lone Pine on U.S. 395, drive east on Highway 136 for 18 miles, and then continue straight on Highway 190 for 30 miles. The right (south) turnoff for Darwin Falls is exactly one mile before you reach the Panamint Springs Resort. Look for a small

Darwin Falls sign and a dirt road. Turn right and drive 2.5 miles on the dirt road to a fork in the road; bear right and park at the signed trailhead. Alternatively, you can exit U.S. 395 at Olancha and Highway 190 and drive east on Highway 190 for 44 miles.

Contact: Death Valley National Park, P.O. Box 579, Death Valley, CA 92328, 760/786-3200, www.nps.gov/deva.

12 WILDROSE PEAK TRAIL
8.4 mi / 5.0 hr   🥾3 △10

in Death Valley National Park

BEST (

If it's boiling in Death Valley, you can always make the long drive out to Wildrose Canyon and begin your hike at a trailhead elevation of 6,800 feet. Get this: You'll even find trees here. Whew, what a relief—at least until you start climbing in earnest, heading for 9,064-foot Wildrose Peak. The hike begins at the 10 charcoal kilns (they look strangely like beehives) that were built in the 1870s to make charcoal for the local mines. Walk to the north end of the kilns to find the signed trail, then start climbing through scattered piñon pines and junipers. You can see far off to the Sierra, even Mount Whitney, and then as you climb higher, you can look down at Death Valley and Panamint Valley. Well-graded switchbacks make the 2,200-foot climb manageable, and the panoramic views make the energy expenditure completely worth it. If you tire out, at least try to hike the first 2.5 miles of trail, where you'll get a good dose of vistas from a saddle below the summit. The last mile to the summit is the steepest.

Special Note: This trail can be snowed in any time between November and May. Check with the park before making the long drive.

User Groups: Hikers and horses. No dogs or mountain bikes. No wheelchair facilities.

Permits: No permits are required. There is a $20 entrance fee per vehicle at Death Valley National Park, good for seven days.

Maps: Free park maps are available at park entrance stations or by contacting Death Valley National Park at the address below. A more detailed map is available from Tom Harrison Maps. For a topographic map, ask the USGS for Wildrose Peak.

Directions: From Stovepipe Wells, drive west on Highway 190 for eight miles to Emigrant Canyon Road, then turn left (south). Drive 21 miles to a junction with Wildrose Canyon Road. Turn left (east) and drive seven miles to the parking area on the right, across from the Charcoal Kilns.

Contact: Death Valley National Park, P.O. Box 579, Death Valley, CA 92328, 760/786-3200, www.nps.gov/deva.

13 GOLDEN CANYON INTERPRETIVE TRAIL
2.0 mi / 1.0 hr 🏃1 ⛰9

in Death Valley National Park

The Golden Canyon Interpretive Trail is a perfect path for first-timers in Death Valley National Park. Because the trail is so short, most people continue beyond the end of the self-guided stretch, heading deeper into Golden Canyon to Red Cathedral, 0.3 mile from the last numbered trail marker. The interpretive trail follows the path of an old road through a flat alluvial fan exhibiting a colorful array of volcanic rocks, sand, and gravel. Imagine every shade of gold you can think of—from yellow to orange to apricot. That's what you'll see here in the cliffs, which are composed of the layered remains of ancient lake beds. They're especially gorgeous near sunrise and sunset. At the final interpretive post, you can turn around and head back, or take the left fork of the trail and continue to Red Cathedral, the huge red cliff that looms in the background. Its lovely hue is caused by the weathering of rocks containing a large quantity of iron. A surprise is that by the time you reach Red Cathedral, you've gained some

300 feet in elevation—enough to provide some wide views looking back the way you came.

User Groups: Hikers only. No dogs, horses, or mountain bikes. No wheelchair facilities.

Permits: No permits are required. There is a $20 entrance fee per vehicle at Death Valley National Park, good for seven days.

Maps: Interpretive trail brochures are available at park visitors centers or at the trailhead. Free park maps are available at park entrance stations or by contacting Death Valley National Park at the address below. A more detailed map is available from Tom Harrison Maps. For a topographic map, ask the USGS for Furnace Creek.

Directions: From the Furnace Creek Visitors Center in Death Valley National Park, drive southeast on Highway 190 for 1.2 miles to the right turnoff for Badwater. Bear right and drive south for two miles to the Golden Canyon parking area, on the east side of the road.

Contact: Death Valley National Park, P.O. Box 579, Death Valley, CA 92328, 760/786-3200, www.nps.gov/deva.

14 GOWER GULCH LOOP
5.5 mi / 3.0 hr 🏃3 ⛰9

in Death Valley National Park

This hike is an extension of Golden Canyon Interpretive Trail (see previous listing) for slightly more experienced hikers. When you reach the last interpretive trail marker on Golden Canyon Trail, take the right fork for Gower Gulch Loop. The path is signed with small hiker symbols; watch for them as you continue your trek into the colorful badlands—deeply creased, eroded, and barren hillsides. Hike across the shoulder of Manly Beacon, a yellow sandstone hill with lovely views. At the base of Manly Beacon's south slope, you reach a junction. Turn right to loop back through Gower Gulch (the left fork leads to Zabriskie Point, a popular drive-to overlook). On your return, remember to stay in the wide main wash and keep heading downhill; this will keep you from making a wrong turn in the canyons of Gower Gulch. You'll notice white outcroppings in the rock, the raison d'être for the old borax mines still found in the area. Also look for mine adits (horizontal shafts); several are bored into the canyon walls. Eventually the canyon narrows, and the trail leads around the side of a 40-foot dry fall. The final mile of the loop parallels the highway, heading back to the mouth of Golden Canyon and its parking area.

One thing to keep in mind: Be sure to carry enough water for the few hours you'll be out on the trail. The total elevation gain is only 800 feet, but it's pretty darn hot out here.

User Groups: Hikers only. No dogs, horses, or mountain bikes. No wheelchair facilities.

Permits: No permits are required. There is a $20 entrance fee per vehicle at Death Valley National Park, good for seven days.

Maps: Free park maps are available at park entrance stations or by contacting Death Valley National Park at the address below. A more detailed map is available from Tom Harrison Maps. For a topographic map, ask the USGS for Furnace Creek.

Directions: From the Furnace Creek Visitors Center in Death Valley National Park, drive southeast on Highway 190 for 1.2 miles to the turnoff for Badwater. Turn right and drive south for two miles to the Golden Canyon parking area, on the east side of the road.

Contact: Death Valley National Park, P.O. Box 579, Death Valley, CA 92328, 760/786-3200, www.nps.gov/deva.

15 TELESCOPE PEAK TRAIL
14.0 mi / 9.0 hr   🏃4 ⛰10

in Death Valley National Park

The chief highlight of the long hike to the summit of Telescope Peak is this: When you get there, you can pivot around and in one

long, sweeping glance take in Mount Whitney to the west and Badwater to the east. For the uninitiated, that means you're seeing the highest point in the contiguous United States and the lowest point in the Western Hemisphere from the same spot (one is ahead of you, one to your back). The other big deal about the hike is that the trailhead is at 8,000 feet, so you don't have to worry about passing out from the valley's heat. The peak (at 11,049 feet) is the highest in Death Valley National Park, and the trail to reach it is well graded and well maintained. Nonetheless, the 3,000-foot climb and the long mileage take their toll, so don't try this hike unless you're in good shape. In addition to passing piñon pines and junipers, you'll also see some ancient bristlecone pine trees once you climb above 10,000 feet. To supplement the vistas of Mount Whitney and Badwater, you are also witness to Death Valley and Panamint Valley, as well as the White Mountains to the north. It's beyond spectacular. But the climb is one heck of a workout, so be prepared.

Special Note: This trail can be snowed in any time between November and May. Check with the park before making the long drive.

User Groups: Hikers only. No dogs, horses, or mountain bikes. No wheelchair facilities.

Permits: No permits are required. There is a $20 entrance fee per vehicle at Death Valley National Park, good for seven days.

Maps: Free park maps are available at park entrance stations or by contacting Death Valley National Park at the address below. A more detailed map is available from Tom Harrison Maps. For a topographic map, ask the USGS for Telescope Peak.

Directions: From Stovepipe Wells, drive west on Highway 190 for eight miles to Emigrant Canyon Road, then turn left (south). Drive 21 miles to a junction with Wildrose Canyon Road. Turn left (east) and drive nine miles to the end of Wildrose Canyon Road at Mahogany Flat Campground. The road gets very rough and steep for the last two miles after the charcoal kilns. High-clearance vehicles are recommended.

Contact: Death Valley National Park, P.O. Box 579, Death Valley, CA 92328, 760/786-3200, www.nps.gov/deva.

16 NATURAL BRIDGE CANYON

1.2 mi / 1.0 hr

in Death Valley National Park

Natural Bridge Canyon is a good spot to take a short walk and get a good taste of what Death Valley is all about. Because the canyon has an abrupt slope, the hike is not as easy as you might expect. The loose gravel surface of its floor makes walking a workout. Still, you should at least go as far as the natural bridge the canyon is named for, which is only 0.3 mile in, or about 15 minutes from your car. The "bridge" is an imposing overhang about 40 feet high and 25 feet wide. It was formed by repeated flash flooding over thousands of years. Take a walk underneath it, then head up the canyon a little farther and watch other visitors walk underneath it. All the while, you can't help but ponder the amazing geologic action that has created Death Valley. If you want to head farther back into the canyon, you'll find more interesting features, such as dry waterfalls and "wax drippings," which are formed when water drips down the canyon walls and forms a type of mud. The canyon walls come together at a 15-foot dry fall 0.6 miles in, so that's your turnaround point.

User Groups: Hikers only. No dogs, horses, or mountain bikes. No wheelchair facilities.

Permits: No permits are required. There is a $20 entrance fee per vehicle at Death Valley National Park, good for seven days.

Maps: Free park maps are available at park entrance stations or by contacting Death Valley National Park at the address below. A more detailed map is available from Tom Harrison

Maps. For a topographic map, ask the USGS for Furnace Creek.

Directions: From the Furnace Creek Visitors Center in Death Valley National Park, drive southeast on Highway 190 for 1.2 miles to the right turnoff for Badwater. Bear right and drive south for 13.2 miles to the left turnoff for Natural Bridge Canyon. Turn left and drive 1.7 miles to the trailhead.

Contact: Death Valley National Park, P.O. Box 579, Death Valley, CA 92328, 760/786-3200, www.nps.gov/deva.

17 FOSSIL FALLS

1.0 mi / 0.5 hr

off U.S. 395 north of the Highway 178 and Highway 14 junction

Now don't get your hopes up and think you're going to find a waterfall way out here in the desert east of U.S. 395. There's no water to be found anywhere at Fossil Falls, but there's an excellent hike to an ancient lava field where you'll find polished and sculptured rock formations. The trail is well maintained, flat, and easy enough for children, although you don't want to hike it at high noon on a hot day. The falls look more like a giant pit or crevice in the ground, carved with beautiful water-sculpted lava formations, which were polished in the last ice age. Fossil Falls is not just appealing to geology buffs; there's something here for history buffs as well: This area was used by Native Americans for at least 10,000 years. There are petroglyphs and rock rings adjacent to the trail. Look and enjoy, but remember that these artifacts are protected by federal law—don't touch or take them.

User Groups: Hikers and dogs. No horses or mountain bikes. No wheelchair facilities.

Permits: No permits are required. Parking and access are free.

Maps: For a topographic map, ask the USGS for Little Lake.

Directions: From the junction of Highway 14

and U.S. 395 near Inyokern, drive north on U.S. 395 for 20 miles to just north of Little Lake, and turn east on Cinder Road. Drive 0.6 mile, bear right at the fork, and drive another 0.6 mile to the Fossil Falls trailhead.

Contact: Bureau of Land Management, Ridgecrest Field Office, 300 S. Richmond Road, Ridgecrest, CA 93555, 760/384-5400, www.ca.blm.gov/ridgecrest.

18 TRONA PINNACLES
0.5 mi / 0.5 hr   🚶1 ⛰8

east of Ridgecrest and south of Trona

If the Trona Pinnacles were miniaturized, they'd look like oblong-shaped lumps of modeling clay ready to be turned on a potter's wheel. They're actually tufa spires made of calcium carbonate, and the Trona Pinnacles National Natural Landmark features more than 500 of them, some as high as 140 feet. Like the tufa spires at Mono Lake, the Trona Pinnacles were formed underwater from calcium-rich springs in the days when giant Searles Lake still had water in it—probably 50,000 years ago. Now the lake bed is dry, so the tufa spires jut upward from a flat, dry plain. Yes, they're weird looking, but in a good way. If you're the kind of person who likes the weird-looking tufa formations at Mono Lake (we are), you'll enjoy this area. A 0.5-mile loop trail leads through the pinnacles, but most people just wander around at random, gazing at the strange, giant tufa spires. Wear sturdy hiking shoes—the tufa is quite sharp.

User Groups: Hikers and dogs. No horses or mountain bikes. No wheelchair facilities.

Permits: No permits are required. Parking and access are free.

Maps: A free brochure on the Trona Pinnacles is available from the Bureau of Land Management at the address below. For a topographic map, ask the USGS for Searles Lake.

Directions: From Ridgecrest, drive east on Highway 178 for 20 miles to the junction

with Trona-Red Mountain Road. Continue on Highway 178 for 7.7 more miles to the signed right turnoff for the trailhead. (High-clearance vehicles are recommended.)

Contact: Bureau of Land Management, Ridgecrest Field Office, 300 S. Richmond Road, Ridgecrest, CA 93555, 760/384-5400, www.ca.blm.gov/ridgecrest.

19 RED CLIFFS
2.0 mi / 1.0 hr   🚶2 ⛰8

in Red Rock Canyon State Park off Highway 14 north of Mojave

Red Cliffs Natural Preserve is a hikers-only section of Red Rock Canyon State Park, where you can walk along and view close up the reddish columns of 300-foot desert cliffs. The color is caused by iron oxide, or rust, but the myriad creases and folds in the cliffs have been formed by a combination of fire and water—volcanic action and the course of streams and rivers. You hike on old jeep tracks, not a formal trail, passing occasional Joshua trees as you go and gaining views of El Paso Mountains. It's hard to believe that this wildernesslike desert is so close to urban Los Angeles, because when you're out here, you feel like you're really far away. At the preserve boundary 0.75 mile from the trailhead, you can continue on the old jeep road into the Scenic Cliffs Preserve or turn around and retrace your steps. The Scenic Cliffs area is closed each year from February 1 to July 1, the nesting season for various birds of prey. If you really want to be wowed, take this hike at sunset, spend the night in the state park campground, and see the stars as you've never seen them before.

User Groups: Hikers, dogs, and horses. No mountain bikes. No wheelchair facilities.

Permits: No permits are required. A $5 day-use fee is charged per vehicle.

Maps: For a topographic map, ask the USGS for Cantil.

Directions: From Mojave, at the junction

of Highways 58 and 14, drive northeast on Highway 14 for about 20 miles to the Red Cliffs parking area, on the right (east) side of the road.

Contact: Red Rock Canyon State Park, 661/320-4001; Mojave Desert Information Center, 43779 15th Street W., Lancaster, CA 93534, 661/942-0662, www.parks.ca.gov.

20 DESERT TORTOISE DISCOVERY LOOP
2.0 mi / 1.0 hr

in Desert Tortoise Natural Area near California City

BEST (

The Desert Tortoise Natural Area features an easy interpretive trail that teaches visitors all about Gopherus agassizii, better known as the desert tortoise, California's state reptile. Don't get your heart set on seeing one, though, as the creatures are rather shy. You have to look for them, and you have to get lucky. At the preserve, you can also learn all about other desert reptiles and desert plants. A few very short interpretive trails are worth strolling, but the two-mile Discovery Trail offers the best chance of seeing tortoises. Look for their burrows underneath creosote bushes, and keep your fingers crossed that one decides to pop his or her head out. Spring (usually from early March to late May) is the best time for tortoise sightings, when the wildflowers are in bloom. The tortoises like to eat them. The best tortoise fact we learned on our trip? During a sudden rainstorm, a tortoise may emerge from its burrow and drink enough water to last a full year.

User Groups: Hikers, horses, and wheelchairs. No dogs or mountain bikes.

Permits: No permits are required. Parking and access are free.

Maps: A free map to the Desert Tortoise Natural Area is available at the trailhead. For topographic maps, ask the USGS for California City North and Galileo Hill.

Directions: From Mojave, at the junction of Highways 58 and 14, drive northeast on Highway 14 for 4.5 miles to California City Boulevard. Drive east on California City Boulevard for nine miles to 20 Mule Team Parkway. Go east on the parkway and continue driving 1.3 miles to Randsburg-Mojave Road. Turn left (northeast) on Randsburg-Mojave Road and drive four miles to the signed parking area.

Contact: Bureau of Land Management, Ridgecrest Field Office, 300 S. Richmond Road, Ridgecrest, CA 93555, 760/384-5400, www.ca.blm.gov/ridgecrest.

21 OWL CANYON / RAINBOW BASIN
4.0 mi / 2.0 hr

northwest of Barstow

You just never know what kind of good stuff you'll find when you travel around the state, and that's certainly true when you reach the Rainbow Basin area north of Barstow. From the Bureau of Land Management's (BLM's) Owl Canyon Campground, you can take a four-mile round-trip hike into some colorful desert country. The well-named Rainbow Basin is made from a cornucopia of colorful sediments—deposits that were formed in lake beds 20 million years ago. The most colorful areas can be seen by taking an auto tour around the basin, but before or after you do so, you should take this hike in Owl Canyon.

The trail begins at Owl Canyon Campground in an ordinary-looking dirt-and-gravel wash. Within minutes, the canyon walls get narrower and rockier, and various colorful sediments begin to show themselves in the rock. There's so much to look at and photograph, and so many boulders and obstacles to climb over and around, that you won't be moving very fast. At 0.6 mile, look for a cave entrance on your right. If you have a flashlight, you can tunnel through it and enter a small side canyon. If you keep traveling in the main canyon, you can hike a total of two miles out. The trail ends near the base of Velvet Peak (a granite ridge), in a colorful rock bowl.

User Groups: Hikers and dogs. No horses or mountain bikes. No wheelchair facilities.

Permits: No permits are required. Parking and access are free.

Maps: For a topographic map, ask the USGS for Mud Hills.

Directions: From I-15 at Barstow, take the Barstow Road exit and drive north 0.8 mile. Turn left on Main Street, drive 0.2 mile, then turn right on First Avenue. Drive one mile, and you will cross over two bridges; just after the second bridge is Irwin Road. Turn left on Irwin Road and drive 5.6 miles. Turn left on Fossil Beds Road (a gravel road), and drive 2.9 miles to the access road for Owl Canyon Campground. Turn right, drive 0.3 mile, then turn right again and drive 1.6 miles to the family campground (go past the group camp). The trail begins by campsite No. 11.

Contact: Bureau of Land Management, Barstow District Office, 2601 Barstow Road, Barstow, CA 92311, 760/252-6000, www.ca.blm.gov/barstow.

22 AFTON CANYON
3.0 mi / 1.5 hr

east of Barstow

They call Afton Canyon "the Grand Canyon of the Mojave," and although its proportions may be smaller than the other Grand Canyon, Afton is no slacker in terms of desert drama. Sheer walls of pink and red rock rise straight up, 300 feet above the Mojave River, where a thin strip of water flows almost year-round. From the campground, follow the trail east along the river, amid a surprising amount of foliage. Saltcedar trees thrive along the stream, as well as planted cottonwoods and willows, creating a protective habitat for birds and other wildlife. As you travel farther, the canyon gets more interesting. Its walls tower above you,

beautifully carved and sculpted by the Mojave River in the days when it was a much bigger waterway—probably 50,000 years ago. Hike as far as you like into the canyon, then turn around and head back. A good side trip is a visit to Pyramid Canyon, one of Afton's side canyons. Start from the campground and cross the river under the first set of railroad trestles, then head south into Pyramid Canyon. The walls slowly narrow until it becomes a classic slot canyon. In the first 0.25 mile, you can see why they call it Pyramid Canyon.

User Groups: Hikers, dogs, horses, and mountain bikes. No wheelchair facilities.

Permits: No permits are required. Parking and access are free.

Maps: For topographic maps, ask the USGS for Cave Mountain and Dunn.

Directions: From Barstow, drive 36 miles east on I-15 and take the Afton Road exit. Drive 3.5 miles southwest to Afton Campground (the dirt road is well graded). Park near the railroad trestles.

Contact: Bureau of Land Management, Barstow District Office, 2601 Barstow Road, Barstow, CA 92311, 760/252-6000, www.ca.blm.gov/barstow.

23 TEUTONIA PEAK
4.0 mi / 2.0 hr

in the Mojave National Preserve east of Barstow

Teutonia Peak on Cima Dome is the perfect summit for geometry enthusiasts. Cima Dome's big claim to fame is that it's the most symmetrical dome of its type in the United States. It rises 1,500 feet above the surrounding landscape, and it covers almost 70 square miles. In fact, the dome is so massive that when you're on top of it, you can't see it.

However, when you're on top of Teutonia Peak, you definitely know you're on it. The peak is at 5,755 feet, and you hike to it via a two-mile trail that leads uphill to head-swiveling desert vistas. The first mile of trail is level and pleasant, leading through cacti, piñon pines, and Joshua trees. Some of the Joshua trees are as tall as 25 feet. (They're a different variety from the kind found in Joshua Tree National Park.) You can clearly see your destination, Teutonia Peak, as well as the rugged-looking New York Mountains in the distance. At 1.5 miles, you start your ascent up the peak. At 1.9 miles, you reach a saddle just shy of Teutonia's summit, where panoramic desert views are revealed. Scramble the last short stretch to reach the summit and catch your breath, enjoying the far-reaching vistas. In winter, you might not stay long, because the wind can howl up here. As you look around, chew on this: The flatlands below are all a part of massive Cima Dome.

User Groups: Hikers, dogs, and horses. No mountain bikes. No wheelchair facilities.

Permits: No permits are required. Parking and access are free.

Maps: A map of Mojave National Preserve is available at the park visitors center. A more detailed map is available from Tom Harrison Maps. For a topographic map, ask the USGS for Cima Dome.

Directions: From Baker, take I-15 east for approximately 25 miles to Cima Road. Turn right (south) on Cima Road and drive 12 miles to the trailhead, on the right side of the road.

Contact: Mojave National Preserve, 2701 Barstow Road, Barstow, CA 92311, 760/252-6100 or 760/252-6108, www.nps.gov/moja.

24 KELSO DUNES

3.0 mi / 1.5 hr

in the Mojave National Preserve southeast of Barstow

What's the most popular place in Mojave National Preserve to watch the sun set? Unquestionably it's Kelso Dunes. Kelso Dunes are the second-highest sand dunes in California.

(Eureka Dunes in Death Valley are the highest.) The dune complex covers 45 square miles, and the dunes reach a height of 700 feet. In a wet spring, desert wildflowers bloom on and around the dunes, adding brighter colors to the gold and pink sand.

Be sure to read the interesting interpretive signs at the Kelso Dunes trailhead, then walk a short distance toward the closest dunes, which are plainly visible. Constantly moving sand makes a formal trail impossible. If you climb high enough in the sand, you are rewarded with views of the surrounding desert, including the Granite and Providence Mountains. Many people don't bother to climb to the top, though. They just plop themselves down and make sand angels or roll around on the dunes' silky surface. Another popular activity is trying to cause small sand avalanches that sometimes produce harmonic booming sounds. For this to occur, the sand must be extremely dry. Some desert lovers swear by the healing power of these vibrating noises.

User Groups: Hikers and dogs. No horses or mountain bikes. No wheelchair facilities.

Permits: No permits are required. Parking and access are free.

Maps: A map of Mojave National Preserve is available at the park visitors center. A more detailed map is available from Tom Harrison Maps. For a topographic map, ask the USGS for Kelso Dunes.

Directions: From Barstow, take I-15 east for approximately 60 miles to Baker, then turn south on Kelbaker Road and drive 42 miles, past Kelso, to the signed road on the right for Kelso Dunes. Turn right (west) and drive three miles to the dunes parking area.

If you are coming from the south on I-40, take the Kelso/Amboy exit and drive 14 miles north on Kelbaker Road to the signed road on the left for Kelso Dunes.

Contact: Mojave National Preserve, 2701 Barstow Road, Barstow, CA 92311, 760/252-6100 or 760/252-6108, www.nps.gov/moja.

25 CRYSTAL SPRINGS TRAIL

1.6 mi / 1.0 hr 🏃3 ⛰9

in the Providence Mountains State Recreation Area southeast of Barstow

The big draw at the Providence Mountains State Recreation Area is touring Mitchell Caverns on a guided walk, so a lot of people miss out on the excellent do-it-yourself hiking trails in the area. The Crystal Springs Trail is the best of those, leading from the visitors center uphill to a rocky overlook in the Providence Mountains. The trailhead elevation is 4,300 feet. The trail is moderately steep—it gains 700 feet over its brief length—and feels surprisingly remote compared to the parking lot full of people waiting to tour the caverns. You hike upward through Crystal Canyon, where lucky hikers sometimes see bighorn sheep. Rocky outcrops shoot up from both sides of the trail. You'll witness a remarkable variety of high-desert foliage: piñon pines, junipers, and prickly plants galore—chollas, barrel cactus, catclaw, cliff rose, and the like. As you climb, keep turning around to check out the increasingly widening vistas. The trail ends near Crystal Springs, where you get a fine view of the surrounding desert and mountains. Then just turn around and head back downhill.

A good side trip is to add a jaunt in the opposite direction from the visitors center. Follow the Niña Mora Overlook Trail from the park campground for 0.25 mile to an overlook of the Marble Mountains and Clipper Valley. And, of course, if you've driven all the way out here, you should sign up for a tour of Mitchell Caverns. The limestone caverns and their stalagmites, stalactites, and helictites are fascinating to see. Tours are held at 1:30 P.M. on weekdays and 10 A.M., 1:30 P.M., and 3 P.M.on weekends and holidays from September through May. In summer, tours are offered at 1:30 P.M. daily.

User Groups: Hikers only. No dogs, horses, or mountain bikes. No wheelchair facilities.

Permits: No permits are required. A $5 day-use fee is charged per vehicle. A $4 fee is charged per adult for a cavern tour ($2 for children ages 6–16; children 5 and under are free but not recommended on the tour). The day-use parking fee is waived with purchase of a cavern tour ticket.

Maps: For a topographic map, ask the USGS for Fountain Peak.

Directions: From Barstow, take I-40 east for 100 miles to the exit for Essex Road, Mitchell Caverns, and Providence Mountains State Recreation Area near the town of Essex. Turn north on Essex Road and drive 15.5 miles to the Providence Mountains visitors center.

Contact: Providence Mountains State Recreation Area, P.O. Box 1, Essex, CA 92332, 760/928-2586, www.parks.ca.gov.

26 ANTELOPE VALLEY POPPY RESERVE LOOP

2.0 mi / 1.0 hr 🏃2 ⛰9

west of Lancaster and Highway 14

BEST (

Our first trip to the Antelope Valley California Poppy Reserve was a wee bit disappointing. We showed up in late March, expecting to see the hillsides completely covered in bright orange flowers, but only a few straggler poppies were left, dry and shriveled from the desert wind. It was our own darn fault for poor planning. If you want to see the magic poppy show at Antelope Valley, you simply must time your trip perfectly. The best way to do so is to call the recorded wildflower update phone line (661/724-1180) or monitor the park website starting in late February; you'll find out exactly when the bloom is expected to be at its best. It can be anywhere from late February to May, and it's different every year. There are several possible loop trips in the park, but the best one for poppy-watching is the North and South Poppy Loop, a combined two-mile loop that leads from the west side of the Jane S. Pinheiro Interpretive Center. Wheelchairs can access a short section of this trail. On either leg of the loop, be sure to take the cutoff trail that leads to the Tehachapi Vista Point, where you can get up high and take a look around.

User Groups: Hikers and wheelchairs. No dogs, horses, or mountain bikes.

Permits: No permits are required. A $5 day-use fee is charged per vehicle.

Maps: For a topographic map, ask the USGS for Del Sur.

Directions: From Lancaster on Highway 14, take the Avenue I exit and turn west on Avenue I, which becomes Lancaster Road. Drive 14 miles to the entrance to the Antelope Valley California Poppy Reserve, on the right. The trail begins by the interpretive center.

Contact: Antelope Valley California Poppy Reserve, 15101 W. Lancaster Road, Lancaster, CA 93536, 661/724-1180, www.parks.ca.gov; Mojave Desert Information Center, 661/942-0662.

27 VASQUEZ ROCKS
3.0 mi / 1.5 hr   🥾2 ⛰️8

in Agua Dulce

In case you're wondering whether there is any "country" left near the city of Los Angeles, the park office at Vasquez Rocks Natural Area should convince you. It's a barn, complete with hay and horses. After stopping by and picking up a trail map, take a walk on the Foot Trail and get a close-up look at the bizarre tilted rock slabs that have made this place famous. (The park has been used in various TV and movie productions.) The largest rock slabs are nearly 150 feet high, and they are tilted as much as 50 degrees, jutting out at various angles toward the sky. The geologic wonders are a result of continuing earth movement along the Elkhorn Fault, which has compressed, folded, and tilted the underlying sandstone rock layers. If you think about it too much, you won't want to stand still in one place for too long. From the parking area, begin hik-

ing on the Foot Trail through the colorful sandstone slabs, then loop back on the Pacific Crest Trail (a dirt road), which returns to the other side of the parking area.

User Groups: Hikers, dogs, horses, and mountain bikes. No wheelchair facilities.

Permits: No permits are required. Parking and access are free.

Maps: Free trail maps are available at the park office. For a topographic map, ask the USGS for Agua Dulce.

Directions: From the junction of I-5 and Highway 14, drive northeast on Highway 14 for 15 miles to Agua Dulce. Take the Vasquez Rocks/Escondido Canyon exit and drive north on Escondido Canyon Road for 2.2 miles to the park entrance. Continue down the dirt road to the large parking lot and picnic area, and begin hiking on the Foot Trail.

Contact: Vasquez Rocks Natural Area, 10700 W. Escondido Canyon Road, Agua Dulce, CA 91390, 661-268-0840, http://parks.co.la.ca.us.

28 SADDLEBACK BUTTE PEAK TRAIL
3.2 mi / 2.0 hr   🥾3 ⛰️9

east of Lancaster and Highway 14

Saddleback Butte State Park is a 3,000-acre Joshua tree woodland, but if those funny-looking trees aren't enough to inspire you to make the trip, this hike to the summit of Saddleback Butte should do it. After a 1,000-foot climb to the 3,651-foot summit, you're rewarded with sweeping vistas of Antelope Valley, the San Gabriel Mountains, the Tehachapi Mountains, and the Mojave Desert. Make sure you've picked a cool day, then start hiking from the park campground through sand and plentiful Joshua trees, heading directly for the clearly visible peak. The first stretch of trail is nearly flat. At one mile out, a trail leads off to the left to Little Butte; ignore it, and continue straight for granite Saddleback

Butte. The last 0.5 mile of trail is remarkably steep and rocky. A saddle near the summit provides excellent views. Keep going to the very top, where you can fully survey the strange surrounding landscape—the meeting place of the western Mojave Desert and the high San Gabriel Mountains.

User Groups: Hikers only. No dogs, horses, or mountain bikes. No wheelchair facilities.

Permits: No permits are required. A $5 day-use fee is charged per vehicle.

Maps: For a topographic map, ask the USGS for Hi Vista.

Directions: From Lancaster on Highway 14, take the 20th Street exit. Drive north on 20th Street for less than 0.5 mile, then turn right (east) on Avenue J. Drive 19 miles on Avenue J to 170th Street East. Turn right, drive one mile, and turn left on Avenue K, at the sign for the state park campground.

Contact: Saddleback Butte State Park, 17102 E. Avenue J, Lancaster, CA 93535, 661/727-9899 or 661/942-0662, www.parks.ca.gov.

29 FORTYNINE PALMS OASIS
3.0 mi / 1.5 hr   2 ⚠8

in Joshua Tree National Park near Twentynine Palms

The biggest surprise on the Fortynine Palms Oasis Trail is not the large and lovely grove of palm trees at the trail's end. It's that there are no Joshua trees to be found anywhere along the trail. What? No Joshua trees in this part of Joshua Tree National Park? It's true—the elevation is a bit too low for them here. Taking their place are the namesake 49 palms, of course, and lovely spring wildflowers, including some orchids growing near the pools in the oasis. Try to hike here in March or April, when you may get lucky and catch the red barrel cacti in bloom. Winter is another lovely season here.

The trail is an old Native American pathway, and it's well maintained and easy to follow.

It winds around, climbs up and over a small ridge, and then curves around to the palm grove. First you'll see a cluster of 10 palms, and then a larger grouping a short distance away. Although you can see and hear Highway 62 and its sprawling suburban towns as you hike, once you reach the palm grove, all traces of civilization are left behind. Have a seat on a boulder to listen and watch for birds. Orioles, finches, and hummingbirds congregate here for both the trickling spring water and the palm fruits. This is a lush, green, vibrant spot, and it is critically important as a watering hole for bighorn sheep and coyotes. The only downer: Some of the beautiful palm trunks have been carved with people's initials.

User Groups: Hikers only. No dogs, horses, or mountain bikes. No wheelchair facilities.

Permits: No permits are required. Parking and access are free in this area of Joshua Tree National Park.

Maps: Free park maps are available at park entrance stations. A more detailed map is available from Tom Harrison Maps or Trails Illustrated. For a topographic map, ask the USGS for Queen Mountain.

Directions: From Banning, drive east on I-10 for 16 miles to the Highway 62 exit. Turn north on Highway 62 and drive 29 miles to the town of Joshua Tree. Continue east on Highway 62 for 10 miles to just west of the town of Twentynine Palms. Turn right (south) on Canyon Road, located by the High Desert Animal Hospital. Drive 1.7 miles on Canyon Road; bear left where the road forks. The pavement ends at the Fortynine Palms Oasis trailhead.

Contact: Joshua Tree National Park, 74485 National Park Drive, Twentynine Palms, CA 92277, 760/367-5500, www.nps.gov/jotr.

HIKING

30 HIGH VIEW NATURE TRAIL
1.3 mi / 1.0 hr 🏃2 ⛰8

In Joshua Tree National Park near Yucca Valley

You're unlikely to have much company on this trail. This lack of popularity, along with its fine vistas and easy grade, is one of its best selling points. The trail is a loop that begins and ends at a parking area near Black Rock Canyon Campground. If you pick up an interpretive brochure at the Black Rock Canyon Nature Center (you'll pass it as you drive in), you can get a brief education on desert plants and animals as you walk. The trail undulates along, climbing a total of only 350 feet, until it reaches a high point with a lovely view of 11,502-foot Mount San Gorgonio and a less-inspiring view of the sprawling desert towns of Yucca Valley and Joshua Tree. A bench marks the spot, and there's a trail register where you can record your comments. The loop back downhill is longer and flatter than the way up. This trail is perfect for a clear winter morning's hike. Note that the loop can also be accessed from the campground and nature center via a 0.5-mile spur trail that begins just west of the nature center.

User Groups: Hikers only. No dogs, horses, or mountain bikes. No wheelchair facilities.

Permits: No permits are required. Parking and access are free in the Black Rock Canyon area of Joshua Tree National Park.

Maps: Free park maps are available at park entrance stations. A more detailed map is available from Tom Harrison Maps or Trails Illustrated. For a topographic map, ask the USGS for Yucca Valley South.

Directions: From Banning, drive east on I-10 for 16 miles to the Highway 62 exit. Turn north on Highway 62 and drive 24 miles to the town of Yucca Valley. Turn right on Joshua Lane (signed for Black Rock Canyon) and drive five miles to the entrance to Black Rock Canyon Campground. Just before the entrance, turn right on a dirt road signed for South Park Parking Area and follow it to its end at the trailhead. The parking area is just outside of the national park boundary, but the trail is inside the park.

Contact: Joshua Tree National Park, 74485 National Park Drive, Twentynine Palms, CA 92277, 760/367-5500, www.nps.gov/jotr.

31 WARREN PEAK
6.0 mi / 3.0 hr 🏃3 ⛰10

In Joshua Tree National Park near Yucca Valley

If you seek a less tame adventure than you get on many short trails in Joshua Tree National Park, the trip to Warren Peak might suit you well. Located in the far northwest corner of the park, the trail and its 5,103-foot summit destination feel surprisingly remote. The peak provides a terrific view of Southern California's tallest mountains, which are crowned with a mantle of snow in winter and early spring. The trail out of Black Rock Canyon Campground starts in a desert wash, with plenty of Joshua trees, piñon pines, and cholla cacti keeping you company. Keep your eyes on the trail signs, which funnel you into the correct forks in the canyon. (There are several critical turns to make.) The sandy wash narrows to a walled canyon, then broadens again. As you climb gently but steadily, you'll see junipers, oaks, and piñon pines replacing some of the lower desert flora. At about two miles out, you'll spy Warren Peak's pointy fractured rock ahead and to the right. The trail gets a bit hard to discern in places, but watch for trail ducks, and keep your eye on Warren Peak. The last 0.25 mile to the summit is steep and requires some scrambling but is easily accomplished. If it's not too windy, you'll want to stay on top of the pointy, conical peak for a while, and not just so you can read the summit register. Views of Mount San Gorgonio, Mount San Jacinto, San Gorgonio Pass, and the Mojave Desert will make your heart pound. To the southwest are Palm Springs and the Morongo and Coachella Valleys.

User Groups: Hikers only. No dogs, horses, or mountain bikes. No wheelchair facilities.

Permits: No permits are required. Parking and access are free in the Black Rock Canyon area of Joshua Tree National Park.

Maps: Free park maps are available at park entrance stations. A more detailed map is available from Tom Harrison Maps or Trails Illustrated. For a topographic map, ask the USGS for Yucca Valley South.

Directions: From Banning, drive east on I-10 for 16 miles to the Highway 62 exit. Turn north on Highway 62 and drive 24 miles to the town of Yucca Valley. Turn right on Joshua Lane (signed for Black Rock Canyon) and drive five miles to the Black Rock Canyon Nature Center. Park and then walk uphill to the Black Rock Canyon trailhead, at the upper end of the campground.

Contact: Joshua Tree National Park, 74485 National Park Drive, Twentynine Palms, CA 92277, 760/367-5500, www.nps.gov/jotr.

32 EUREKA PEAK
10.8 mi / 6.0 hr   3 10

in Joshua Tree National Park near Yucca Valley

The total elevation gain on this trip is only 1,500 feet to reach the summit of Eureka Peak (at 5,518 feet), but it feels more difficult than that. The problem is sand and rocks—lots of them—and the fact that the trail is hard to discern in places. However, if you're willing to put in some effort, your reward is a commanding view of the western edge of Joshua Tree National Park, as well as Mount San Jacinto and Mount San Gorgonio. Sand and snow—you see it all from here. Begin hiking on the California Riding and Hiking Trail, which you'll follow for two miles until you come to a major wash. This is where things start to get tricky; keep looking for trail markers

signed as EP (for Eureka Peak) to keep you on track. Take the right fork in the wash, leaving the California Riding and Hiking Trail. In another 0.5 mile, take the next right fork into another wash. Hike through this wash for 1.7 miles to its end. A trail marker directs you to your left, heading up and over a ridge. At the top, turn right (south), hike up to a saddle, and then continue on to the south side of Eureka Peak, where there's a short path to the summit. When you get to the top, what's the only downer? You find that plenty of people have driven their cars up to the peak via a dirt road from Covington Flat. No fair. An option is to follow this road back downhill for one mile to the California Riding and Hiking Trail, turn left, and follow the trail back to your starting point. It makes a good loop trip and only adds one mile to your total distance.

User Groups: Hikers only. No dogs, horses, or mountain bikes. No wheelchair facilities.

Permits: No permits are required. Parking and access are free in the Black Rock Canyon area of Joshua Tree National Park.

Maps: Free park maps are available at park entrance stations. A more detailed map is available from Tom Harrison Maps or Trails Illustrated. For topographic maps, ask the USGS for Yucca Valley South and Joshua Tree South.

Directions: From Banning, drive east on I-10 for 16 miles to the Highway 62 exit. Turn north on Highway 62 and drive 24 miles to the town of Yucca Valley. Turn right on Joshua Lane (signed for Black Rock Canyon) and drive five miles to the Black Rock Canyon Nature Center. Park at the nature center and then walk uphill to the California Riding and Hiking Trail trailhead, on the left (east) side of the campground entrance.

Contact: Joshua Tree National Park, 74485 National Park Drive, Twentynine Palms, CA 92277, 760/367-5500, www.nps.gov/jotr.

HIKING

33 BARKER DAM LOOP

1.5 mi / 1.0 hr

in Joshua Tree National Park near Twentynine Palms

There's a lake in the desert (well, in wet years, anyway), and it's hidden in a magical place called the Wonderland of Rocks. You can't water-ski or fish there, but you can enjoy bird-watching and photograph the reflections of odd-shaped boulders in the water's surface. The lake was last seen in 1998, before a series of dry years hit Southern California, but with a few good winter rains, it will be back. When it exists, the lake is formed by Barker Dam, built at the beginning of the 20th century to improve upon a natural boulder dam that captured rain runoff in this basin. Even if the lake is only a mirage when you visit, this short loop is still a great walk, as it also leads past many of the unique granite boulders of the Wonderland of Rocks. Rock climbers can often be seen strutting their stuff here. The trail loops back past some petroglyphs (take the short spur trail) and Indian grinding holes. If the petroglyphs seem remarkably visible and clear to you, it's because years ago a movie crew painted over them to make them more visible to the camera. For this tragic reason, the park calls these paintings the "Disney petroglyphs."

User Groups: Hikers only. No dogs, horses, or mountain bikes. No wheelchair facilities.

Permits: No permits are required. There is a $15 entrance fee per vehicle at Joshua Tree National Park, good for seven days.

Maps: Free park maps are available at park entrance stations. A more detailed map is available from Tom Harrison Maps or Trails Illustrated. For a topographic map, ask the USGS for Indian Cove.

Directions: From Banning, drive east on I-10 for 16 miles to the Highway 62 exit. Turn north on Highway 62 and drive 29 miles to the town of Joshua Tree. Turn right on Park Boulevard and drive 14 miles to Hidden Valley Campground, on the left. Follow the signs for Barker Dam.

Contact: Joshua Tree National Park, 74485 National Park Drive, Twentynine Palms, CA 92277, 760/367-5500, www.nps.gov/jotr.

34 RYAN MOUNTAIN TRAIL

3.0 mi / 2.0 hr

in Joshua Tree National Park near Twentynine Palms

BEST (

If you hike only one trail in Joshua Tree National Park, this should be the one. Ryan Mountain (at 5,470 feet) provides what many insist is the best view in the park. You can see the Queen Valley, Wonderland of Rocks, Lost Horse Valley, Pleasant Valley, and the far-off mountains, San Gorgonio and San Jacinto. It's a complete panorama. The route travels through boulders and Joshua trees—no surprises here—on a well-maintained and easy-to-follow trail. The ascent is a bit steep—a 1,000-foot elevation gain over only 1.5 miles—but it's over with quickly, so just sweat it out. Be sure to sign the summit register and then have a seat on one of the rocks of Ryan Mountain to enjoy the view. The peak's boulders are estimated to be several hundred million years old, which gives you something to think about while you admire the vista.

User Groups: Hikers only. No dogs, horses, or mountain bikes. No wheelchair facilities.

Permits: No permits are required. There is a $15 entrance fee per vehicle at Joshua Tree National Park, good for seven days.

Maps: Free park maps are available at park entrance stations. A more detailed map is available from Tom Harrison Maps or Trails Illustrated. For a topographic map, ask the USGS for Keys View.

Directions: From Banning, drive east on I-10 for 16 miles to the Highway 62 exit. Turn north on Highway 62 and drive 45 miles to Twentynine Palms and the park visitors center.

Turn right on Utah Trail Road and drive eight miles to a Y junction. Bear right and continue for nine miles, past Sheep Pass Campground to the trailhead parking area, on the south side of the road. You can also reach the trailhead via Park Boulevard out of the town of Joshua Tree, turning left at Cap Rock Junction and continuing 2.5 miles to the trailhead.

Contact: Joshua Tree National Park, 74485 National Park Drive, Twentynine Palms, CA 92277, 760/367-5500, www.nps.gov/jotr.

35 SKULL ROCK NATURE TRAIL
1.7 mi / 1.0 hr 🏃1 ⛰7

in Joshua Tree National Park near Twentynine Palms

Joshua Tree National Park is arguably more famous for its rock formations than it is for Joshua trees. If you want a close look at some of the park's weird and wonderful hunks of quartz monzonite, the Skull Rock Trail will provide it. The official trail is only 0.25 mile long, but if you're okay with doing a little cross-country hiking, you can easily turn it into a 1.7-mile loop. The trail provides a quick education: Interpretive signs point out paper-bag bush, turbinella oak, cholla cactus, and other desert flora. The path runs between the Skull Rock parking area and Loop E in Jumbo Rocks Campground, so you can start at either place. It winds among giant, rounded rock formations and passes by its namesake, Skull Rock. The big boulder looks loosely like what its name implies. A spiderweb of paths leads around Skull Rock; this is where everyone abandons the formal trail and starts climbing around on the smooth, rounded rock surfaces. To complete the longer loop, you must cross the park road twice, navigate an unmaintained stretch on the north side of the road, and walk a 0.5-mile stretch of the Jumbo Rocks Campground entrance road. It sounds complicated, but it's quite doable.

User Groups: Hikers only. No dogs, horses, or mountain bikes. No wheelchair facilities.

Permits: No permits are required. There is a $15 entrance fee per vehicle at Joshua Tree National Park, good for seven days.

Maps: Free park maps are available at park entrance stations. A more detailed map is available from Tom Harrison Maps or Trails Illustrated. For a topographic map, ask the USGS for Malapai Hill.

Directions: From Banning, drive east on I-10 for 16 miles to the Highway 62 exit. Turn north on Highway 62 and drive 45 miles to Twentynine Palms and the park visitors center. Turn right on Utah Trail Road and drive eight miles to a Y junction. Bear right and continue four miles to the trailhead parking area alongside the road shortly before the entrance to Jumbo Rocks Campground. Begin hiking on the left (south) side of the road. If you are camping at Jumbo Rocks, you can start hiking from the entrance to Loop E.

Contact: Joshua Tree National Park, 74485 National Park Drive, Twentynine Palms, CA 92277, 760/367-5500, www.nps.gov/jotr.

36 LOST HORSE MINE
4.2 mi / 2.0 hr 🏃2 ⛰8

in Joshua Tree National Park near Twentynine Palms

You get the full desert experience on the Lost Horse Mine Trail, including spectacular mountain and valley vistas, high-desert flora, and a visit to an old gold mine. The trail (really an old road) leads uphill for 1.8 miles to Lost Horse Mine. The mine produced a gold profit at the turn of the century—9,000 ounces of gold—and is the best preserved of all the mines in the national park. Still standing are the mine's stamp mill, old building foundations, and a few open mine shafts. Continue from the mine another 0.3 mile up the old road, climbing more steeply up the ridge to wide overlooks of the Queen Valley, Lost

Horse Valley, Pleasant Valley, and the eastern stretch of the national park. The summit here is 5,278 feet; turn around and retrace your steps before the trail begins to descend.

User Groups: Hikers only. No dogs, horses, or mountain bikes. No wheelchair facilities.

Permits: No permits are required. There is a $15 entrance fee per vehicle at Joshua Tree National Park, good for seven days.

Maps: Free park maps are available at park entrance stations. A more detailed map is available from Tom Harrison Maps or Trails Illustrated. For a topographic map, ask the USGS for Keys View.

Directions: From Banning, drive east on I-10 for 16 miles to the Highway 62 exit. Turn north on Highway 62 and drive 29 miles to the town of Joshua Tree and Park Boulevard. Turn right on Park Boulevard and drive 15.8 miles to Cap Rock junction. Bear right and drive 2.4 miles to the dirt road on the left that is signed for Lost Horse Mine. Turn left and follow the dirt road to the trailhead parking area.

Contact: Joshua Tree National Park, 74485 National Park Drive, Twentynine Palms, CA 92277, 760/367-5500, www.nps.gov/jotr.

37 MASTODON PEAK
3.0 mi / 1.5 hr   👥2 ⛰9

in southern Joshua Tree National Park near Cottonwood Spring

BEST (

The Mastodon Peak Trail begins at Cottonwood Spring Oasis, a little slice of watery paradise for birds and wildlife. After a short paved section, the trail sets off in the desert sand, and after 0.5 mile, you take the left fork for Mastodon Peak. Shortly you'll pass another trail junction with the path to Cottonwood Spring Campground; stay right. The route has almost no elevation change along its route to the base of the peak. It's a pleasant, easy stroll among tall ocotillos, yucca, and smaller cacti. At the Mastodon's base, you must choose whether or not to scramble to the top; the

going is steep but short. Although it's a nice trip just to hike to the peak's base and try to imagine the Mastodon's profile, it's recommended you go for the summit. The easiest route is around the back of the Mastodon, on its east side. In a few minutes you are at the top, admiring the surprisingly wide view: Not only do you see a great expanse of Joshua Tree's desert and the Eagle Mountains, but also snowcapped Mount San Jacinto and the miragelike Salton Sea shimmering in the distance some 30 miles away.

If you want to add some history to your hike, retrace your steps to the junction with the trail to Cottonwood Spring Camp. Turn right there and hike past the Mastodon Gold Mine and the Winona Mill Site. The mine was worked in the 1920s with a modicum of success. From the mill site, you don't need to backtrack to the main trail; the path loops back to the Cottonwood Spring parking area.

User Groups: Hikers only. No dogs, horses, or mountain bikes. No wheelchair facilities.

Permits: No permits are required. There is a $15 entrance fee per vehicle at Joshua Tree National Park, good for seven days.

Maps: Free park maps are available at park entrance stations. A more detailed map is available from Tom Harrison Maps or Trails Illustrated. For a topographic map, ask the USGS for Cottonwood Spring.

Directions: From Indio, drive east on I-10 for approximately 25 miles. Turn north on Cottonwood Spring Road and drive seven miles to Cottonwood Spring visitors center. Turn right and drive another mile, passing the campground entrance, to the day-use parking area at Cottonwood Spring Oasis.

Contact: Joshua Tree National Park, 74485 National Park Drive, Twentynine Palms, CA 92277, 760/367-5500, www.nps.gov/jotr.

38 LOST PALMS OASIS

7.5 mi / 3.5 hr   👥2 ⛰9

in southern Joshua Tree National Park near
Cottonwood Spring

BEST (

If the weather is cool and accommodating
and you're in the mood for a longer hike in
southern Joshua Tree National Park, the Lost
Palms Oasis Trail comes highly recommended.
Many consider Lost Palms Oasis to be the
best palm grove in Joshua Tree, and the hike
to reach it has little elevation change. The
trail begins at Cottonwood Spring Oasis and
for the first 0.5 mile follows the same path as
the Mastodon Peak Trail. Stay straight at the
junction with the trail to Mastodon Peak; continue straight through a series of washes and
low ridges covered with various low-elevation
desert cacti. There is no indication of the huge
palm oasis until you are almost on top of it, at
slightly more than three miles out. The main
trail brings you to an overlook point above
the palms, and a steep use trail descends 0.25
mile into the grove. Make the rugged 200-foot
descent to the canyon bottom; the remoteness
of the area and the lush atmosphere of the leafy
palm grove make it worth the effort. The Lost
Palms Oasis grove contains more than 100
palms in its main canyon. In the upper end of
the canyon is a side canyon with more palms,
although these are more difficult to reach.

User Groups: Hikers only. No dogs, horses, or
mountain bikes. No wheelchair facilities.

Permits: No permits are required. There is
a $15 entrance fee per vehicle at Joshua Tree
National Park, good for seven days.

Maps: Free park maps are available at park
entrance stations. A more detailed map is
available from Tom Harrison Maps or Trails
Illustrated. For a topographic map, ask the
USGS for Cottonwood Spring.

Directions: From Indio, drive east on I-10 for
approximately 25 miles. Turn north on Cottonwood Spring Road and drive seven miles
to Cottonwood Spring visitors center. Turn
right and drive a mile, past the campground

entrance, to the day-use parking area at Cottonwood Spring Oasis.

Contact: Joshua Tree National Park, 74485
National Park Drive, Twentynine Palms, CA
92277, 760/367-5500, www.nps.gov/jotr.

39 BIG MORONGO CANYON LOOP

1.5 mi / 1.0 hr   👥1 ⛰8

in the Big Morongo Canyon Preserve north of
Palm Springs

Big Morongo Canyon Preserve is a bird-
watcher's place, plain and simple. In fact, if
you're not carrying binoculars and a field book
when you visit, you'll feel like a real outsider.
Fortunately, you don't have to know anything
about birds to have a good time. We exam-
ined the interpretive exhibit at the trailhead
kiosk, and within a few minutes of hiking, we
were able to spot and identify a pair of western
tanagers. (And usually we can't tell a blue jay
from a blue grouse.) The best bird-watching
seasons are spring and fall, so time your trip
for those times if possible. Although a fire
burned through this preserve in June 2005,
consuming much of the willows and riparian
plants, the vegetation is quickly returning.

Start this loop from the kiosk by bearing
left to connect to the Desert Willow Trail,
an exposed pathway through a desert wash,
then in 0.4 mile turn left again on the Yucca
Ridge Trail. As you climb Yucca Ridge, you'll
gain panoramic views of Big Morongo Canyon and the San Jacinto and San Gorgonio
Mountains. Note the gneiss and schist rock
formations along the trail; they are some of the
oldest rocks in California—one to two billion
years old. In 0.7 mile, connect to the Mesquite
Trail and enjoy a streamside walk alongside
Fremont cottonwoods and red willows that are
regenerating after the 2005 fire. You may smell
the distinct scent of sulfur from underground
springs. Finally you'll join the Marsh Trail for
the final stint back to the trailhead, follow-

HIKING

ing a boardwalk made of recycled plastic milk containers. If you haven't added a few species to your bird list by this point in the hike, you will now. More than 1,400 pairs of birds per square kilometer nest here annually, making the Marsh Trail a bird-watcher's paradise.

User Groups: Hikers only. No dogs, horses, or mountain bikes. Wheelchair users can follow the fully accessible Marsh Trail.

Permits: No permits are required. Parking and access are free.

Maps: For a topographic map, ask the USGS for Morongo Valley.

Directions: From Banning, drive east on I-10 for 16 miles to the Highway 62 exit. Turn north on Highway 62 and drive 11 miles to Morongo Valley. Look for a sign on the right for the Big Morongo Canyon Preserve (at East Drive); turn right and drive 200 yards to the preserve entrance, on the left. Trails begin at the kiosk/information center.

Contact: Big Morongo Canyon Preserve, P.O. Box 780, Morongo Valley, CA 92256, 760/363-7190, www.bigmorongo.org.

40 AERIAL TRAMWAY TO DESERT VIEW TRAIL

2.0 mi / 1.0 hr 🏃1 ⛰10

in Mount San Jacinto State Park and Wilderness

The first time you ride the Palm Springs Aerial Tramway, you realize that human beings are capable of creating miracles. In just a few minutes (which you spend gaping out the big windows at the view), you are whooshed from the desert floor, at 2,643 feet in elevation, to the Mount San Jacinto State Park and Wilderness, at 8,516 feet. From cacti to clouds, from palms to pines, and in our case, from desert heat to snow flurries. There are dozens of possible hikes from the top of the tramway, but the easiest of them all is on the Desert View Trail. Since the trail is in the state park but not in the state wilderness, you don't even need a

permit—just get off the tram and start hiking. Where else for so little effort can you get expansive views of the desert and high mountain country? Not too many places.

To reach the Desert View Trail, follow the park's nature trail to the left from the back of the tram station; it joins Desert View. The vistas are awesome every step of the way, especially looking out over Palm Springs and the Indian Canyons. As you walk, be on the lookout for Cooper's hawks and yellow-rumped warblers.

Here's an insider's tip for planning your trip: The best deal on the Palm Springs Aerial Tramway is to buy the Ride and Dine Ticket (available after 3 P.M.). For a moderate additional charge, you get a huge buffet dinner to go with your tram ride and day of exploring on the mountain. It's an incredible experience to spend the afternoon hiking, have dinner in the huge dining room as the sun goes down, and then ride the tram back downhill in the darkness.

User Groups: Hikers only. No dogs, horses, or mountain bikes. No wheelchair facilities.

Permits: No permits are required. The Palm Springs Aerial Tramway charges $21.95 per adult and $14.95 per child ages 3–12 for a round-trip ticket to Mountain Station. Contact the Palm Springs Aerial Tramway for information about schedules, fees, and special programs.

Maps: A trail map of Mount San Jacinto State Park and Wilderness is available at the offices listed below. For a topographic map, ask the USGS for San Jacinto Peak.

Directions: From Banning, drive 12 miles east on I-10 and take the Highway 111/Palm Springs exit. Drive nine miles south on Highway 111 to Tramway Road, then turn right and drive 3.5 miles to the tramway parking area. Walk to the tram station, buy your ticket, and ride the tram to its end at Mountain Station. Walk out the back side of Mountain Station, follow the paved path downhill, and walk to your left for the Desert View Trail.

Contact: Mount San Jacinto State Park and

Wilderness, P.O. Box 308, 25905 Highway 243, Idyllwild, CA 92549, 951/659-2607, www.parks.ca.gov; Palm Springs Aerial Tramway, 760/325-1391 or 888/515-8726, www. pstramway.com.

⁴¹ AERIAL TRAMWAY TO SAN JACINTO PEAK
11.6 mi / 6.6 hr

in Mount San Jacinto State Park and Wilderness

 BEST (

You could hike to 10,834-foot San Jacinto Peak the hard way, upward from Idyllwild on one of several possible trails, but then you'd miss out on the many delights of the Palm Springs Aerial Tramway and hiking through Long and Round Valleys. So take the tram instead, get your wilderness permit at the ranger station, and begin hiking on the Round Valley Trail. It switchbacks gently uphill through the pines and firs, most of the time following a creek laden with corn lilies, to reach beautiful Round Valley, at 9,100 feet. At the west end of Round Valley, you reach a Y in the trail, near the seasonal ranger station. Take the left fork heading toward Wellmans Divide, with a short, steep ascent just before you reach it. The views to the north and east are inspiring, including jagged Tahquitz Peak and Red Tahquitz—a bit of foreshadowing of things to come.

At the divide, turn right on the Deer Springs Trail. You have 2.6 miles to go, and the views stay with you the whole way. Climb northward on the granite slopes of Miller Peak, make a sharp left switchback, and head southwest to the spur trail for San Jacinto Peak, on the right. Once you're on the spur, it's only a few hundred yards to the peak, where the views are truly breathtaking. You can see just about all of Southern California, even into Mexico and Nevada, and out to the Pacific Ocean. John Muir said that the vista from San Jacinto was "one of the most sublime spectacles

seen anywhere on Earth," and he was a guy who saw a lot of vistas. Total elevation gain is 2,300 feet.

User Groups: Hikers only. No dogs, horses, or mountain bikes. No wheelchair facilities.

Permits: A free wilderness permit is required for day hiking or backpacking in the San Jacinto Wilderness and is available from the ranger station at Mountain Station. Backpackers should obtain a permit in advance by mail from Mount San Jacinto State Park and Wilderness at the address below. The Palm Springs Aerial Tramway charges $21.95 per adult and $14.95 per child ages 3–12 for a round-trip ticket to Mountain Station. Contact the Palm Springs Aerial Tramway for information about schedules, fees, and special programs.

Maps: A trail map of Mount San Jacinto State Park and Wilderness is available at the offices listed below. A map of the San Jacinto Wilderness is available from Tom Harrison Maps. For a topographic map, ask the USGS for San Jacinto Peak.

Directions: From Banning, drive 12 miles east on I-10 and take the Highway 111/Palm Springs exit. Drive nine miles south on Highway 111 to Tramway Road, then turn right and drive 3.5 miles to the tramway parking area. Walk to the tram station, buy your ticket, and ride the tram to its end, at Mountain Station. Walk out the back side of Mountain Station, follow the paved path downhill, and head right (west) for a few hundred yards to the ranger station. Get a day-hiking permit and continue hiking on the well-signed trail heading for Round Valley.

Contact: Mount San Jacinto State Park and Wilderness, P.O. Box 308, 25905 Highway 243, Idyllwild, CA 92549, 951/659-2607, www.parks.ca.gov; Palm Springs Aerial Tramway, 760/325-1391 or 888/515-8726, www. pstramway.com.

HIKING

42 MURRAY CANYON TRAIL

4.0 mi / 2.0 hr

on the Agua Caliente Indian Reservation in Palm Springs

If you think Palm Springs is all tennis courts, golf courses, and beauty parlors, you haven't been to the Indian Canyons off South Palm Canyon Drive. The Indian Canyons—Palm, Andreas, and Murray—are what's left of the old Palm Springs. They're wide-open stretches of desert, with red rock, fan palms, sulfur streams, barrel cactus, bighorn sheep, and broad vistas of surprising color and beauty. The Murray Canyon Trail is an excellent exploration of this area, beginning at the picnic grounds between Murray and Andreas Canyons. The trail is well-packed sand and is clearly marked along the way. After an initial wide-open desert stretch, you enter Murray Canyon, which narrows and twists and turns, so you never see where you're going until you come around the next bend. The stream you've been following begins to exhibit a stronger flow, and the streamside reeds, grasses, palm trees, and wild grapes intensify their growth accordingly. If you're a fan of red rock, you'll love the 100-foot-tall slanted rock outcrops and cliffs. After passing a left fork for the Caufmann Trail, climb up and over a small waterfall in Murray Canyon, staying on the left side of the stream. In another 0.25 mile, you'll reach a larger set of falls. These falls block any possible further progress but provide many good pools for swimming and granite shelves for picnicking.

One thing to keep in mind when you visit Murray Canyon, or any of the Indian Canyons: Make sure you check what time the park gates are closing for the day, and then make sure you finish your hike so your car is out of the parking lot by closing time. Show up 15 minutes late, and you can have a real problem on your hands. (Guess how we know.)

User Groups: Hikers and horses. No dogs or mountain bikes. No wheelchair facilities.

Permits: No permits are required. An $8 day-use fee is charged per adult; $4 for children 6–12.

Maps: A brochure and trail map are available at the entrance kiosk. For topographic maps, ask the USGS for Palm Springs and Cathedral City.

Directions: From Palm Springs, drive south through the center of town on Highway 111/Palm Canyon Drive and take the right fork signed for South Palm Canyon Drive. Drive 2.8 miles, bearing right at the sign for Palm Canyon/Andreas Canyon. Stop at the entrance toll gate, drive about 200 yards, and turn right for Murray Canyon. Drive past the Andreas Canyon trailhead and continue to Murray Canyon Picnic Area, a mile from the entrance kiosk.

Contact: Palm Springs Visitors Center, 2777 N. Palm Canyon Drive, Palm Springs, CA 92256, 760/416-7044.

43 TAHQUITZ CANYON

2.0 mi / 1.0 hr

on the Agua Caliente Indian Reservation in Palm Springs

BEST (

Just about everything in Palm Springs has a legend behind it, and Tahquitz Canyon (pronounced TAW-kits) is no exception. Named for an Agua Caliente Indian shaman who abused his powers and was banished from his tribe, Tahquitz Canyon is a spectacular outdoor museum of desert flora and fauna. Yet the curse of Tahquitz remains so powerful that even today, some local tribe members refuse to venture into the evil shaman's rock-studded canyon.

Not so for the thousands of Palm Springs visitors who have hiked here since Tahquitz Canyon's public reopening in 1999. After years of abuse by raucous, partying crowds in the 1960s and 1970s, the canyon was closed to public access for more than two decades. The Agua Caliente Indians, owners of this land, took great pains to clean out all the garbage, graffiti, and debris and to restore this desert canyon to its native state. Now visitors can join a guided hike or walk on their own along this easy trail through the canyon to the base of its 60-foot waterfall. Movie buffs will recognize the showering falls as the entrance to the land of Shangri-La in Frank Capra's 1937 film Lost Horizon. Tahquitz's other treasures include plentiful bird life, Indian rock art, and lush stands of desert lavender, mesquite, and creosote. Don't miss a trip to this unique place; it is sure to be the highlight of your visit to Palm Springs.

User Groups: Hikers only. No dogs, horses, or mountain bikes. No wheelchair facilities.

Permits: Fees are $12.50 per adult and $6 for children 12 and under. Reservations are recommended for guided tours.

Maps: For topographic maps, ask the USGS for Palm Springs and Cathedral City.

Directions: From Palm Springs, drive south through the center of town on Highway 111/Palm Canyon Drive and turn right on Mesquite Avenue. Drive 0.5 mile to the Tahquitz Canyon visitors center. The guided hike begins here.

Contact: Tahquitz Canyon Visitors Center, 500 W. Mesquite Avenue, Palm Springs, CA 92256, 760/416-7044.

44 BORREGO PALM CANYON
3.0 mi / 1.5 hr

in Anza-Borrego Desert State Park near Borrego Springs

BEST (

The hike to Borrego Palm Canyon Falls is only 1.5 miles in length, but it feels like a trip from the desert to the tropics. You start out in a sandy, rocky, open plain, sweating it out with the cacti and ocotillo, and you end up in a shady oasis of fan palms, dipping your feet in the pool of a fern-covered waterfall. The trip begins on the Borrego Palm Canyon Trail from the state park campground, where you should top off your water bottles and start walking. If you pick up an interpretive brochure at the park visitors center, you can identify the array of desert plants that grow along the trail, including cheesebush, brittle-bush, catclaw (ouch!), and chuparosa. In 0.5 mile, when you pass interpretive post 20, you're suddenly surprised by the sight of bright green, leafy palm trees up ahead. Borrego Palm Canyon is home to more than 800 mature native palms, the largest of more than 25 groves in the park. It's one of the largest oases in the United States. Head toward the palms, and in a few minutes, you'll be nestled in their shade, listening to the desert wind rustle their fronds. Follow the trail a little farther, and you'll reach a 15-foot waterfall that streams over giant boulders and forms a large, sandy pool tucked in among the palms. We saw many maidenhair ferns growing by the water's edge and a tiny hummingbird flitted about the scene. Ah, paradise.

User Groups: Hikers only. No dogs, horses, or mountain bikes. No wheelchair facilities.

Permits: No permits are required. A $6 day-use fee is charged per vehicle.

Maps: A map of Anza-Borrego Desert State Park is available at the park visitors center. An Anza-Borrego Desert State Park map is also available from Tom Harrison Maps. For a topographic map, ask the USGS for Borrego Palm Canyon.

Directions: From Julian, drive east on Highway 78 for approximately 19 miles to Highway S3/Yaqui Pass Road. Turn left (north) on Highway S3/Yaqui Pass Road and drive 12 miles to Borrego Springs. Turn left on Highway S22/Palm Canyon Drive and drive one mile to the signed junction just before the park visitors center. Turn right and drive one mile to Borrego Palm Canyon Campground. The trailhead is at the west end.

Contact: Anza-Borrego Desert State Park, 200 Palm Canyon Drive, Borrego Springs, CA 92004, 760/767-5311, www.parks.ca.gov; visitors center, 760/767-4205.

45 MAIDENHAIR FALLS

5.0 mi / 3.0 hr   ₃ ▲₉

in Anza-Borrego Desert State Park near Hellhole Canyon

If you have taken the hike to Borrego Palm Canyon Falls and found that it suited your taste for desert adventure, this trip to Maidenhair Falls is a more challenging path to a slightly bigger and more dramatic desert waterfall. Stop in at the park visitors center before you begin, and pick up a handout with trail directions. Also remember to be prepared for a longer excursion in the desert (bring tons of extra water, and cover your head with a light-colored hat). Your destination is a 20-foot waterfall with a walled backdrop of maidenhair ferns and mosses. The route to reach it travels from Highway S22 south of the visitors center into the mouth of Hellhole Canyon. Begin on the California Riding and Hiking Trail for the first 200 yards and turn right. You'll pass a few fan palms, myriad cacti, some odd-shaped rocks, and Native American grinding holes along the route. Cottonwoods grow in places along the stream. Maidenhair Falls is a bit tricky to find, tucked into a narrow canyon corner, but with luck, there will be enough water running in the stream to clue you in to its location.

User Groups: Hikers only. No dogs, horses, or mountain bikes. No wheelchair facilities.

Permits: No permits are required. Parking and access are free.

Maps: A map of Anza-Borrego Desert State Park is available at the park visitors center. An Anza-Borrego Desert State Park map is also available from Tom Harrison Maps. For a topographic map, ask the USGS for Tubb Canyon.

Directions: From Julian, drive east on Highway 78 for approximately 19 miles to Highway S3/Yaqui Pass Road. Turn left (north) on Highway S3/Yaqui Pass Road and drive for 12 miles to Borrego Springs. Turn left on Highway S22/Palm Canyon Drive and drive

one mile to the signed junction just before the park visitors center. Turn left and drive 0.75 mile to the large parking lot on the west side of the road.

Contact: Anza-Borrego Desert State Park, 200 Palm Canyon Drive, Borrego Springs, CA 92004, 760/767-5311; visitors center, 760/767-4205, www.parks.ca.gov.

46 CACTUS LOOP AND YAQUI WELL

2.75 mi / 1.5 hr   ₂ ▲₈

in Anza-Borrego Desert State Park near Tamarisk Grove

The Cactus Loop and Yaqui Well Trails are two separate nature trails at Anza-Borrego Desert State Park, but since they're right beside each other, you might as well hike both. The Cactus Loop Trail is a 0.75-mile loop, and more hilly than you might expect from a nature trail. It shows off seven kinds of cacti, including barrel, hedgehog, fishhook, beavertail, and cholla. Visitors often spot chuckwallas and other lizards scurrying among the spiny plants. The Yaqui Well Trail climbs for one mile among cacti, ocotillo, and cholla to a mesquite grove and then reaches Yaqui Well. In a small circle around this seep, a tremendous variety of greenery grows, including mesquite and false desert willow, given life by the year-round presence of water. Desert birds show up here, particularly colorful hummingbirds. If you're in the mood for more desert education, drive five miles east of Tamarisk Grove to the short little loop trail at the Narrows. It's packed with a lot of geologic punch; you'll get a big lesson in geological processes, from faulting and landslides to erosion and earthquakes.

User Groups: Hikers only. No dogs, horses, or mountain bikes. No wheelchair facilities.

Permits: No permits are required. Parking and access are free.

Maps: A map of Anza-Borrego Desert State

Park is available at the park visitors center. An Anza-Borrego Desert State Park map is also available from Tom Harrison Maps. For a topographic map, ask the USGS for Borrego Sink.

Directions: From Julian, drive east on Highway 78 for 19 miles to Tamarisk Grove Campground at Road S3. The trailheads for the Cactus Loop and Yaqui Well Trails are opposite the camp entrance off Road S3.

Contact: Anza-Borrego Desert State Park, 200 Palm Canyon Drive, Borrego Springs, CA 92004, 760/767-5311; visitors center, 760/767-4205, www.parks.ca.gov.

47 PICTOGRAPH TRAIL

2.0 mi / 1.0 hr

in Anza-Borrego Desert State Park near Blair Valley

Although a Native American rock-art site is the destination of this trip, the Pictograph Trail comes with a bonus: an inspiring overlook of the Vallecito Mountains from the brink of a dry waterfall. It's a desert vista that's hard to forget. The path begins at the Pictograph trailhead and wanders through huge granite boulders. First you head through a dry wash and then climb up a ridge. At 0.5 mile out, you begin to descend. At 0.75 mile, you'll find some pictographs, painted in red and yellow pigments by the nomadic Kumeyaay Indians. (Look for the pictographs on the side of a boulder on the right side of the canyon.) The slightly faded geometric designs were made with natural pigments and are estimated to be 2,000 years old. Continue farther on the trail, and the canyon narrows dramatically until its walls come together at the brink of a dry waterfall more than 150 feet tall. From its edge the panoramic view is stunning, both of the steep dropoff and the far-off mountains and valley.

User Groups: Hikers only. No dogs, horses, or mountain bikes. No wheelchair facilities.

Permits: No permits are required. Parking and access are free.

Maps: A map of Anza-Borrego Desert State Park is available at the park visitors center. An Anza-Borrego Desert State Park map is also available from Tom Harrison Maps. For a topographic map, ask the USGS for Earthquake Valley.

Directions: From Julian, drive east on Highway 78 for 12 miles to Road S2, turn south, and drive six miles to the left turnoff for Blair Valley Camp. Turn left (east), drive 1.4 miles on a dirt road, and then bear right at the fork. Drive another 1.6 miles and bear left at the next fork. In 0.25 mile, bear left again. Continue two more miles to the end of the road, at the Pictograph trailhead.

Contact: Anza-Borrego Desert State Park, 200 Palm Canyon Drive, Borrego Springs, CA 92004, 760/767-5311; visitors center, 760/767-4205, www.parks.ca.gov.

48 ELEPHANT TREE TRAIL

1.5 mi / 1.0 hr

in Anza-Borrego Desert State Park near Split Mountain

It's not just the odd-looking elephant tree that you get to see on this trail, but also many of the common flora of Anza-Borrego Desert—creosote bush, burroweed, indigo bush, barrel cactus, ocotillo, catclaw, cholla, smoke tree. … There's enough desert-plant identification to do to keep you quizzing your hiking partner all day. But it's the single elephant tree on the loop that steals the show, with its crinkled, folded "skin" on its trunk. The tree is an odd patchwork of colors (yellowish bark, blue berries, and orange twigs) and its bark has a very evocative odor, something like a spicy air freshener. The Elephant Tree Trail used to feature several elephant trees, but all but this one lone specimen have died. It is located near the end of the loop. If possible, time your trip for early spring, when the ocotillos sprout brilliant red plumes and the pink sand verbenas bloom.

User Groups: Hikers only. No dogs, horses, or mountain bikes. No wheelchair facilities.

Permits: No permits are required. Parking and access are free.

Maps: A map of Anza-Borrego Desert State Park is available at the park visitors center. An Anza-Borrego Desert State Park map is also available from Tom Harrison Maps. For a topographic map, ask the USGS for Harper Canyon.

Directions: From Julian, drive east on Highway 78 for 35 miles to Ocotillo Wells. Turn south on Split Mountain Road and drive 5.8 miles to the right turnoff that is signed for Elephant Trees. Turn right and drive 0.8 mile on a dirt road to the trailhead.

Contact: Anza-Borrego Desert State Park, 200 Palm Canyon Drive, Borrego Springs, CA 92004, 760/767-5311; visitors center, 760/767-4205, www.parks.ca.gov.

49 GHOST MOUNTAIN TRAIL
2.0 mi / 1.0 hr 🏃3 ⛰9

in Anza-Borrego Desert State Park near Blair Valley

When most people imagine a life of living off the land, they instinctively think of doing so in a place where water is plentiful. Not so with Marshal South, who in the 1930s chose Ghost Mountain, in the Anza-Borrego Desert. South and his wife built an adobe home atop the mountain and lived there with their children for more than 15 years. The family tried to live simply, attempting to survive in the spartan style of early Native Americans. Sadly, South's wife eventually tired of the rugged desert life and her husband's odd idealism, and the family split up.

The Ghost Mountain Trail climbs through a series of switchbacks to the remains of the South homesite, which includes a few partial walls, an old mattress frame, and some assorted

cisterns and barrels used for storing precious water. The destination is worthwhile not just because the sight of it sparks your imagination, but also because of the lovely, 360-degree desert views you gain as you ascend Ghost Mountain. When you stand on the top on a clear, cool day, you can almost imagine why South chose this remote homesite.

Remember that Blair Valley and Ghost Mountain are higher in elevation than other parts of the park. Not only does this make them cooler spots for hiking, but it also means that a wide variety of desert plant life grows here. The ocotillos and yuccas put on a spectacular show in early spring.

User Groups: Hikers only. No dogs, horses, or mountain bikes. No wheelchair facilities.

Permits: No permits are required. Parking and access are free.

Maps: A map of Anza-Borrego Desert State Park is available at the park visitors center. An Anza-Borrego Desert State Park map is also available from Tom Harrison Maps. For a topographic map, ask the USGS for Earthquake Valley.

Directions: From Julian, drive east on Highway 78 for 12 miles to Road S2, turn south, and drive six miles to the left turnoff for Blair Valley Camp. Turn left (east), drive 1.4 miles on a dirt road, and then bear right at the fork. Drive another 1.6 miles, bear right again, and drive 0.5 mile to the Ghost Mountain/Marshal South Home trailhead.

Contact: Anza-Borrego Desert State Park, 200 Palm Canyon Drive, Borrego Springs, CA 92004, 760/767-5311; visitors center, 760/767-4205, www.parks.ca.gov.

50 MOUNTAIN PALM SPRINGS CANYON
2.6 mi / 2.0 hr

in Anza-Borrego Desert State Park near Bow Willow

Although the groves of fan palms in Mountain Palm Springs Canyon are not as large as in Borrego Palm Canyon, they're still beautiful and popular with park visitors. The palm oases, fed by underground springs and shaded by the magnificent fan palms, create a haven for plants and wildlife, as well as for hikers looking for a cool and pleasant place to spend the day. Six distinct palm groves grow in Mountain Palm Springs Canyon, as well as occasional elephant trees; you can visit all of the groves in one walk. The trail doesn't look like much to start, just a rocky arroyo, but it gets more trail-like in short order. The first grove of trees, Pygmy Grove, has been burned. The second grove, Southwest Grove, is larger and prettier. Take the right fork just before you enter Southwest Grove and head uphill to an elephant tree and the one-mile path to the Surprise Canyon Grove. From Surprise Canyon, you can turn left to see Palm Grove Bowl—it's a natural bowl that is ringed with more than 100 palm trees. Return to Surprise Canyon and loop back to your starting point, passing by North Grove on the way. Or retrace your steps to Southwest Grove and take the short spur to the southwest to see Torote Bowl. There are some good elephant tree specimens there. If you visit in early winter when the palms bear their fruit (dates), you may find so many birds singing in the palm trees that you can hardly hear yourself think. Look for the pretty hooded oriole in particular, which builds its nest on the underside of palm fronds.

User Groups: Hikers only. No dogs, horses, or mountain bikes. No wheelchair facilities.

Permits: No permits are required. Parking and access are free.

Maps: A map of Anza-Borrego Desert State Park is available at the park visitors center. An Anza-Borrego Desert State Park map is also available from Tom Harrison Maps. For a topographic map, ask the USGS for Sweeney Pass.

Directions: From Julian, drive east on Highway 78 for 12 miles to Road S2, turn south, and drive 29 miles to the Mountain Palm Springs Campground entrance road, on the right. Turn right and drive straight for 0.6 mile (don't take any of the campsite turnoffs) to the parking area by a stone marker for Mountain Palm Springs Canyon.

Contact: Anza-Borrego Desert State Park, 200 Palm Canyon Drive, Borrego Springs, CA 92004, 760/767-5311, www.parks.ca.gov; visitors center, 760/767-4205.

51 ROCK HILL TRAIL
2.0 mi / 1.5 hr

on the east shore of the Salton Sea near Calipatria

If it's wintertime—anywhere from December to February—it's a good time to pay a visit to the Salton Sea National Wildlife Refuge (now called the Sonny Bono Salton Sea National Wildlife Refuge, after the 1970s singer-turned-politician), one of the lowest places in the United States, at 228 feet below sea level. Winter is the only season when the area isn't blistering hot, and it's also the time that peak populations of birds are gathered at the refuge. The place has one hiking trail, called the Rock Hill Trail, which gets hiked by approximately 40,000 bird-watchers a year. From the observation platform behind the visitors center, the path heads out along a levee and then abruptly climbs to a hill above the Salton Sea. It's a great place to watch the pelicans dive and to shake your head in wonder at the immense size of the saline Salton Sea. The sea was formed from 1905 to 1907, when a series of artificial dams on the Colorado River burst their seams. Its water has become increasingly saline over the years due to agricultural runoff, evaporation, and the lack of a replenishing freshwater supply.

Although fish do not fare well in the changing waters of the Salton Sea, bird lovers find plenty to cheer about. In addition to seeing the plentiful waterfowl that spend the winter in the saltwater and freshwater marshes—geese of many kinds, mergansers, widgeons, and teals—hikers might spot an endangered species such as the Yuma clapper rail or peregrine falcon. Migrating snow geese and Ross geese are also big attractions along this trail. They are seen in great numbers every December.

User Groups: Hikers only. No dogs, horses, or mountain bikes. No wheelchair facilities.

Permits: No permits are required. Parking and access are free.

Maps: A free map of the refuge is available at the visitors center. For a topographic map, ask the USGS for Niland.

Directions: From Indio, drive south on Highway 111 for approximately 50 miles to the turnoff for Sinclair Road, which is four miles south of Niland. (If you reach Calipatria, you've gone too far.) Turn right on Sinclair Road and drive six miles to the Salton Sea National Wildlife Refuge visitors center, located at the intersection of Sinclair Road and Gentry Road.

Contact: Sonny Bono Salton Sea National Wildlife Refuge, 906 W. Sinclair Road, Calipatria, CA 92233, 760/348-5278, http://pacific.fws.gov/salton.

52 NORTH ALGODONES DUNES WILDERNESS
1.0 mi / 1.0 hr 　 2 　 8

east of Brawley and south of the Salton Sea

The Algodones Dunes could best be described as an ocean of sand. They are located in the far southeast corner of California, amid a whole lot of... well, to be honest, nothing. Still, this is a unique and fragile place, where a massive dune system covers more than 1,000 square miles. In between the dunes lie flat basins in which desert willow, smoke trees, and mesquite flourish. Rare reptiles, such as the desert tortoise and fringe-toed lizard, make their homes here. In fact, this is such a fragile environment that permits are required for all visitors. The only time to visit the dunes is between October and April, because it is as hot as Hades the rest of the year. Summer days are typically over 120 degrees. The dunes rise to heights of 350 feet and stretch over a five-mile-wide expanse. You can wander around as much as you like, but since walking in sand is a trying experience, you probably won't wander very far. (There are no formal trails across the dunes because of the continually shifting sands.) Mostly, this is a place to visit to gain a glimpse into a rare, special world comprised entirely of sand and sky.

User Groups: Hikers, dogs, and horses. No mountain bikes. No wheelchair facilities.

Permits: Permits are required for parking and access; visit www.blm.gov/ca/st/en/fo/elcentro.html for permit information.

Maps: A brochure and trail map are available from the Bureau of Land Management (BLM) office listed below. For a topographic map, ask the USGS for Niland.

Directions: From Brawley, drive east on Highway 78 for 26 miles. The wilderness area lies on the north side of the highway, but it is illegal to park alongside the road. Instead, park at the Watchable Wildlife Area north of Highway 78 on the Niland-Glamis Road (along the west side of the railroad tracks). If your visit will be 30 minutes or less, you can park at the Osborne Overlook on Highway 78 (a permit is not required if you park here).

Contact: Bureau of Land Management (BLM), El Centro Field Office, 1661 S. Fourth Street, El Centro, CA 92243, 760/337-4400, www.blm.gov/ca/st/en/fo/elcentro.html.

Index

California Deserts Hiking

MOON CALIFORNIA DESERTS CAMPING & HIKING

Avalon Travel
a member of the Perseus Books Group
1700 Fourth Street
Berkeley, CA 94710, USA
www.moon.com

Editor and Series Manager: Sabrina Young
Copy Editor: Michelle Peters
Graphics Coordinator: Kathryn Osgood
Production Coordinator: Elizabeth Jang
Cover Designer: Kathryn Osgood
Interior Designer: Darren Alessi
Map Editor: Kevin Anglin
Cartographers: Kat Bennett, Chris Markiewicz
Proofreader: Erika Howsare

ISBN: 978-1-59880-279-5

Text © 2009 by Tom Stienstra,
Ann Marie Brown.
Maps © 2009 by Avalon Travel.
All rights reserved.

ABOUT THE AUTHORS

Tom Stienstra

For 30 years, Tom Stienstra's full-time job has been to capture and communicate the outdoor experience. This has led him across California – hiking, boating, fishing, camping, biking, and flying – searching for the best of the outdoors and then writing about it.

Tom is the nation's top-selling author of outdoors guidebooks. He has been inducted into the California Outdoor Hall of Fame and has twice been awarded National Outdoor Writer of the Year, newspaper division, by the Outdoor Writers Association of America. He has also been named California Outdoor Writer of the Year five times, most recently in 2007. Tom is the outdoors columnist for the *San Francisco Chronicle*; his articles also appear on www.SFGate.com and in newspapers around the country. He broadcasts a weekly radio show on KCBS-San Francisco and hosts an outdoor television show on CBS/CW San Francisco.

Tom lives with his wife and sons in Northern California. You can contact him directly via the website www.tomstienstra.com. His recent guidebooks include:

Moon California Camping
Moon California Fishing
Moon California Recreational Lakes and Rivers
Moon Northern California Cabins & Cottages
Moon Northern California Camping
Moon Oregon Camping
Moon Pacific Northwest Camping
Moon Washington Camping
Moon West Coast RV Camping

Ann Marie Brown

The author of 13 outdoor guidebooks, Ann Marie Brown is a dedicated California outdoorswoman. She hikes, bikes, and camps more than 150 days each year in a dedicated effort to avoid routine, complacency, and getting a real job.

Ann Marie's work has appeared in *Sunset*, *VIA*, *Backpacker*, and *California* magazines. As a way of giving back a little of what she gets from her experiences in nature, she writes and edits for several environmental groups, including the Sierra Club and the Natural Resources Defense Council. When not traipsing along a California trail, Ann Marie can be found at her home near South Lake Tahoe. Ann Marie's recent guidebooks include:

Moon 101 Great Hikes of the San Francisco Bay Area
Moon Bay Area Biking
Moon Northern California Biking
Moon Tahoe
Moon Take a Hike Los Angeles
Moon Yosemite

For more information on these titles, visit Ann Marie's website, www.annmariebrown.com.